Praise for
Stand Up to Workplace Bullying and Discrimination

"Chock-full of personal stories, practical strategies, and priceless nuggets, this workbook will empower you to stand up to the bullies in your workplace. A must-read for anyone being taken advantage of by people in power."

–**Jeff Riggenbach**, *PhD, International Speaker/Trainer/Coach*
with the John Maxwell team

"Dawn's knowledge and support helped me navigate a toxic work environment. After a year of passive-aggressive behavior, micromanaging, and verbal abuse I resigned from the position. I owe Dawn a debt of gratitude for helping me realize no job is worth sacrificing your well-being. I now know what to do if I ever work in a toxic work environment again.

–**Barb McKenzie**, *EdD, Behavioral Consultant*

"We all deserve (and have the right) to work in a respectful workplace environment free from bullying, discrimination, and incivility. There is simply no place for these negative elements in the workplace. Unfortunately, however, not all workplaces live up to that ideal, and the employees ultimately pay the price. Dawn walks us through what bullying in the workplace looks like—and carefully explains in plain and simple terms how bullying differs from discrimination and harassment. The workbook is chock-full of useful templates, checklists, and samples that employees can use to advocate for themselves in difficult and uncomfortable situations.

Having spent more than 30 years as a management-side employment lawyer, human resources executive, and champion for respectful and civil workplaces, I recommend Dawn's workbook and most heartily endorse it as required reading for anyone who feels that they are not being treated appropriately at work."

–**Keith Black**, *Esquire; Principal of Employment Practices Outsourcing*

Stand Up to Workplace Bullying and Discrimination

Solutions, Tools, & Guidelines

Dawn Marie Westmoreland

MM/HRM, CPC, CH

LYSTRA BOOKS
& Literary Services

ISBN 978-1-7363055-3-9
Library of Congress Control Number: 2021909476

Poem, "Prayer for Peace," used with the kind permission of its author, Michael Lancaster

Author's photograph by April Johnson

Book design by Kelly Prelipp Lojk

LYSTRA BOOKS
& Literary Services

Publication managed by
Lystra Books & Literary Services, LLC
Chapel Hill, NC
lystrabooks@gmail.com

 CONTENTS

Preface vii

Acknowledgments x

About This Workbook xi

Empowerment Pledge to Yourself xiii

1 Building Your Confidence and Courage 1

2 Bullying in the Workplace 19

3 The Persona of a Bully 27

4 Statistics and Guidance on Workplace Bullying and Discrimination 35

5 Employment Discrimination in the Workplace 45

6 More Protected Discrimination Classes and Stories 58

7 Documenting Your Workplace Bullying or Discrimination Matter 69

8 Rest, Recovering, and Healing Modalities 84

9 Programs That Can Support You During a Workplace Issue 99

Resources to Help You 107

Epilogue 118

Endnotes 119

Notes 122

 **PREFACE**

I wrote the *Everything You Need to Know About Standing Up to Bullying and Discrimination* workbook to empower men and women who want to know how to conquer workplace bullying or discrimination. If you are reading this book, you may need some help. You may be supporting a mistreated person. Congratulate yourself on taking a step to help yourself or another person.

In my book, *The Empowered Whistleblower*, I discussed my story of standing up to workplace bullying and discrimination. I had blown the whistle on what I felt were prohibited personnel practices in my former government agency in 2012. My federal employee coworkers were following me to the lady's bathroom to ask questions about the validity of our managers hiring their friends and family. What ensued was severe bullying and retaliation because I spoke up for myself and others who had worked alongside me.

I was falsely charged with allegations and placed on over 100 days of administrative leave. My managers accused me of Absence Without Leave (AWOL), which could have gotten me fired from my federal job. I stopped receiving paychecks because I was not provided with a Reasonable Accommodation to be able to work from home due to my "disabilities." I also had to sell my beautiful home in South Asheville, NC, because I could no longer afford to live in it. I chose to downgrade to a house I could afford at the time. My credit scores went from outstanding to poor because I could not pay all my bills. As I pursued my discrimination case against the Department of Veteran Affairs, my paychecks were cut off as a retaliatory action.

After suffering emotionally and financially for a year, I received a formal hearing date for my case. I learned to be more resilient and courageous during that year. I decided to refuse to sign a nondisclosure agreement so that I could share my story, but most of all, so I could help others. Upon settling with the Department of Veteran Affairs (VA), two days before the EEOC formal hearing, I knew I had gone through my journey to teach others all the lessons and insights I gained from my experience.

Working nearly thirty years in Human Resources has enabled me to share solutions to create safe and respectful work environments. To empower others, I became a certified Life Coach. It can be immensely helpful to have a mentor guiding you. Gratefully, a handful of great mentors supported me as I recovered from an ugly experience and began to thrive on helping other people. I honorably retired from the United States Air Force after twenty years in 2005. I have learned a lot about leadership and resiliency that I will share with you.

No matter how strong you think you are, everyone has a breaking point when they are mistreated for long periods of time. I was not a weak female; it took a lot of harassment to make me weak and pass out two times at work. I was taken by ambulance to the Asheville VA Hospital for medical care both times. Even though my physical and mental health were declining, I knew I was going through all my experiences for a good reason. Life became even more empowering after I decided to help others who have been bullied and discriminated against in their workplaces.

It's been gratifying to create my podcast, *The Empowered Whistleblower*, that provides resources, guidance, and more to listeners. There is nothing more exciting than helping others who want civility in the workplace. I was asked to be a radio talk host on work issues with Asheville, North Carolina's WPVM FM 103.7. I set the intention of evolving my work and meeting Erin Brockovich in May of 2017, and I interviewed her on my podcast in 2018. A world-famous activist and former legal clerk, Erin helped build a case against Pacific Gas and Electric Company (PG&E) in 1993 for contaminated water. Julia Roberts portrayed Erin in the movie, *Erin Brockovich*.

There have been many guests on my podcast and radio show who have offered ways to handle stress, anxiety, depression, leadership solutions, and accountability. Employment attorneys have provided legal counseling, and other experts have filled in the gaps with knowledge and strategies to help people overcome the trauma of being mistreated. In 2015, I spoke to numerous senators and their staffs on the need to protect employees from workplace bullying and discrimination.

The Concerned Veterans for America sent me and one hundred others to Washington DC to talk to thirty senators about VA whistleblowers and other concerns. I also became a columnist with the Good Men Project (www.goodmenproject.com), sharing stories about my work to help men and women. Their website receives up to four million views each month and discusses current and past topics. I joined in with a thousand other writers who shared articles about ethics, politics, advice, confessions, and much more. Some of my articles "trended" and were noted as the top ten articles of the day.

Great things continued to happen for me after I decided to help others. *The Christian Science Monitor* correspondent, Lisa Susay lauded me for turning a bad situation into something good for others. I provided advice on a 2018 TV special in Charlotte, NC, on Solutions to Workplace Bullying and

Discrimination. It reinforced the idea that people are looking for respect and civility where they work.

In 2018, I served as a subject matter expert and a board member for "respectful work environments" in Philadelphia. On numerous occasions I have been a panelist expert to share my knowledge of workplace mistreatment. Quite a few doors opened with possibilities for my work to expand, and I chose wisely. Employees spend up to one-third of their lives working. They deserve to work in a safe and respectful work environment.

While I have the experience and credentials to provide guidance and insights to support you, an employment attorney is qualified to help you with employment laws. Also, when needed, a mental health professional is highly recommended for support. Please use sound judgment in selecting the right legal counsel and medical professionals. They can be highly instrumental in helping you, along with my guidance.

Prayer for Peace

As there is no greater hand than love, so there is none worse than violence, harming a child, a woman, an elder, an animal, all defenseless against the blow. Even the shouted word is violent, always unnecessary even to the speaker. Let us pledge a deep change. Turn your heart away from violence as your means. Become rather a hand of help and kindness, love, gentleness.

Be you at peace. Give your peace away.

– Michael Lancaster

Michael has dedicated this poem to his son, Scott Lancaster, who has served traumatized kids and helped run a domestic violence shelter for 26 years.

❧ ACKNOWLEDGMENTS

I am incredibly grateful to Martha Juchnowski who has been a loyal, compassionate mentor to me for many years. I have transformed into a more empowered person with her guidance and wisdom. Blaine Greenfield has graciously mentored me on marketing and has been a sage business advisor. He has been my greatest cheerleader and keeps me smiling. Thanks to Edward Blomgren, Ph.D., Ryan McShane, Deb Sinness Drummond, Meredith Brown, Tracy Crow, Meredith Brown, and Barb McKenzie for being my beta readers.

Edward Blomgren, Ph.D. gave me the idea to create a "empowerment pledge." I worked with three terrific female military veterans for nearly two years as we helped to improve each other's writing—Tracy Crow, Meredith Brown, and Deb Sinness Drummond. Tracy Crow read my manuscripts and provided outstanding guidance on producing quality books. Meredith Brown and Deb Sinness Drummond have told me what I needed to hear for making this a helpful workbook.

My friend and go-to Workplace Violence Security Consultant, Felix Nater reviewed my book and provided some very insightful guidance that has been added to this workbook. My mother, Patricia Goss, has never given up on me and has always been my rock. She has been an inspiration, conquering breast cancer and beating all the odds. Each person has mentored me and supported my writing, business, and ability to help others. They inspired me and motivated me to write this workbook.

🌿 ABOUT THIS WORKBOOK

This is the first comprehensive workbook on bullying and discrimination in the workplace. I have carefully outlined this workbook with strategies that helped me when I was bullied and discriminated against in the workplace. If you want to get the most out of this workbook, read it thoroughly. You have made an especially important decision in reading and applying the strategies in this workbook. Chances are good that you will become more empowered, confident, and educated. This workbook is a compilation of two years' work and research. Life is too long not to be happy!

Facing your fears or experiencing mistreatment in the workplace can be uncomfortable. You deserve to be congratulated for deciding to help yourself or another person. Real change requires effort and time. Be patient with yourself and tell yourself, "things always work out for the best for me." Willingness and determination can go far when you follow the steps in this workbook.

Remember, you always deserve to be treated with respect and work in a safe work environment. No matter how small or big of a problem you may be facing—the solutions are likely in this workbook. There are other books on bullying and discrimination, however, this workbook offers:

🍃 Comprehensive guidance and strategies to deal with mistreatment in the workplace.

🍃 Guidance on building your confidence and courage.

🍃 An explanation of the persona of a bully.

🍃 Statistics and guidance on bullying and discrimination in the workplace.

🍃 Other people's stories of bullying and discrimination (victories and losses).

🍃 Step-by-step strategies to document negative work incidents.

🍃 Modalities, personnel programs and more to help with your physical and mental health.

🍃 How "resistance" can impact your personal growth and how to stand up for yourself.

🍃 Resources, in addition to this workbook, to help you if you are being bullied or discriminated against.

NOTE: *While it may be tempting to skip around in this workbook, it is possible that you could miss important, helpful information. That is what this book is about: helping you to stand up to bullying and discrimination.*

❧ EMPOWERMENT PLEDGE TO YOURSELF

Today, (DATE) _____, and forevermore, I hereby pledge to myself that I will no longer accept bullying or discrimination in my life, and in my workplace. I have the right to work in a safe and respectful work environment. I promise to do my best in making decisions that empower me. I value my work ethics and how I am treated in the workplace.

I promise to:

🍃 help myself by taking care of my physical and mental health.

🍃 understand I cannot change other people, but I can change myself.

🍃 properly document workplace incidents involving bullying or discrimination.

🍃 consider the merit of moving to a different job, if needed

🍃 hold my antagonist accountable, if willing and possible, through court or the Equal Employment Opportunity Commission, or other resources

🍃 respect and honor my feelings; they are valid.

🍃 know that I am a worthy person, deserving to work in a safe and respectful work environment.

🍃 protect myself when treated unacceptably or inappropriately.

🍃 team up with professionals such as an employment attorney or mental health professional, if needed.

_____

SIGN

CHAPTER ONE

Building Your Confidence and Courage

This chapter discusses:

- Confidence, courage, and finding your strength
- Budgeting your finances for confidence
- Stories of others who have been bullied
- Resources

David and Goliath

Are you familiar with the biblical story of David and Goliath? The account of David and Goliath is not only a popular story; it is a reminder of courage, overcoming adversity, and faith. The Israelites were called upon to fight the Philistine army that had gathered for the war. A young shepherd boy named David was tired of hearing Goliath mocking Israel and their God, so he pled with King Saul to let him fight Goliath.

David stands up to the nine-foot giant, Goliath. David, dressed in the garb of a shepherd, has only a slingshot and a rock. The giant, heavily armed, has a spear and sword. Goliath will surely slaughter David the "underdog." The mighty giant also had a full suit of armor for the fight. However, after listening to Goliath laugh at him, David hurls a rock in his sling. The rock makes a direct hit on the giant, who falls to the ground. The humble shepherd boy cut off Goliath's head, and that changed history. David's faith and confidence won the battle that day.

Why was a humble shepherd victorious that day? David had the advantage as the underdog. Shepherds must keep their sheep from predators because they provide milk for cheese and wool for material. Most shepherds were nomadic and had to be quick on their feet to prevent attacks on their flock. A simple slingshot and confidence were often all the shepherds needed to protect his sheep. You may have a situation in your job where you may feel like "David" facing a "Goliath." Malcolm Gladwell's book, *David and Goliath*, inspired me to write this chapter.

If you are going through any kind of mistreatment in the workplace, you may need someone to help guide you through this workbook. You are not weak for asking for support; you are wise to reach out and ask for help. Even strong people can use a little help when dealing with workplace issues. If you need someone who can help you go through this workbook, mental health professionals have the experience to support you. If this is not an option, consider finding a person capable of helping you because they are a strong person or may have overcome their own past trauma. These are some of your best resources to help guide you through this workbook.

Because the word "bully" may trigger you and cause emotional distress. I will substitute the word "antagonist" for "bully" in some of the workbook. I will replace the word "victim" with "target" in some instances in this workbook because most people do not like to be called a victim.

Confidence and Courage Checklist

Place a check by each statement that describes or is similar to your experience in the workplace.

☐ 1. Do you feel that you need to love and respect yourself more?

☐ 2. Do you feel you need healthy boundaries or restrictions with everyone in your life?

☐ 3. Do you feel that you need help with displaying a confident composure or behavior?

☐ 4. Do you feel like you focus on your weaknesses rather than your strengths?

☐ 5. Do you feel like you can't move forward in your life due to harassment?

☐ 6. Do you find yourself saying "yes" to things you don't want to do in your life?

If you checked even one of these statements, it's an opportunity to work on being more confident and courageous. If you checked one or two, you may have experienced bullying. If you checked three to five on this checklist, you are definitely being bullied. Last, if you have checked more than five on this checklist, you are experiencing "extreme bullying."

Resistance Can Only Conquer You If You Yield to It

It can be uncomfortable standing up to people who act mean. While some people may hope their workplace bullying or discrimination issue goes away, it often does not. For many people, personal growth requires being uncomfortable at times. You may be afraid or uncomfortable becoming more empowered. Your "inner voice" may tell you to stay safe, be quiet, and accept mistreatment. However, if you genuinely want to be liberated, at peace, and more joyful, you have to get out of your comfort zone.

I have never met anyone who enjoyed being mistreated, demeaned, or discriminated against in the workplace. We all need psychological safety in the workplace where we feel safe, accepted, and even respected. We want the leadership in a company to validate our concerns and take appropriate action when we are harmed by people who mistreat us. It's a very reasonable request and one that everyone deserves. Personal growth is something we all need because it's the path to a better life. A life where we are treated as valued employees has a ripple effect on other parts of our lives.

When you go home from work, you want to spend time with the people you love, your pets, and enjoy a peaceful sanctuary. Even if you are single, you want to enjoy the sweet things in your life. The good thing is that you get to decide what level of personal growth you want to achieve. Steven Pressfield is my favorite author on resistance. In his book, *Turning Pro*, Pressfield states, "What we get when we turn pro is, we find our power. We find our will and our voice, and we find our self-respect." I like Steven Pressfield a lot. He tells it like it is and that is what many influencers do; they share their humiliating stories, how they overcame, and how they are helping others today.

As you go through this workbook, you may feel a range of unnerving emotions, even though this workbook was written to support you. It's easy to get distracted with other things in your life to avoid supporting yourself. For example, you may hope your workplace issues will go away and want to take no action to help yourself. You may not want to put a lot of effort into standing up for yourself because it makes you uneasy. If you find yourself "resisting" these steps, it may be because it feels awkward to become a more empowered person. It's ok. Acknowledge how you feel inside and move forward. Push through your fears and become a stronger, more confident person.

This workbook is going to take you from an amateur to a pro on standing up to workplace bullying and discrimination. I promise you if you follow, heed, and apply the advice given in this workbook, you will likely become an empowered employee and a professional expert on standing up for yourself in the workplace.

The "C" Words—Confidence and Courage

If you have been bullied or discriminated against, your confidence can take a blow from the experience. All the clients I worked with felt their confidence or courage took a big dip. You may have also experienced trauma or mistreatment in your workplace. Worrying about being fired, demoted, or paying your bills can traumatize even a strong, confident person.

Even I felt hopeless, discouraged, and insecure for a while. Years ago, I needed a "Reasonable Accommodation" from my managers after being released by the Asheville VA hospital, and my managers denied me the right to work out of my home. I needed to be able to find a way to accomplish my work duties with the disabilities I had at the time. The Americans with Disability Act of 1990 (ADA) is a civil rights law that prohibits discrimination based on disability. I was financially broke from the loss of income from the VA, and I became deeply depressed, knowing that I couldn't afford the lifestyle I had worked hard for and had been enjoying. At the time, I was living in a large home in South Asheville, NC. In a matter of months, I could not pay my bills, resulting in delinquency with my financial responsibilities. I was divorced and had taken on some of the bills formerly shared between myself and my former spouse, Mark.

Since I lost around 60 percent of my income because the Veteran Affairs refused to let me work from home, the loss of my financial stream meant I had to sell my beautiful house quickly, cut out all traveling for pleasure, and stop eating out at restaurants. I even sold about 70 percent of the nice items in my former home to pay bills, which was difficult and sometimes impossible. I take financial responsibilities very seriously, so this was the saddest period for me, as my credit score and financial portrait were compromised.

At first, I found it hard selling all my possessions from my former home. Houses were not selling very well because of the depressed market, and it took nearly eight months to sell. I often heard that someone wanted to buy my house, but they had bad credit scores from the economic crisis we all had experienced. Finally, after the house sold, I moved to a smaller home within my budget.

Of all the harm used to break me, watching my outstanding credit scores reduced to poor scores was humiliating, and the saddest time of my life. But—it was not the end of the world. In my case, I learned how to live on a tight budget and be more creative. You may inevitably face hardships and struggle in your life, but how you perceive your experience can help you grow and become a more confident person. One of the things that always gets someone's attention is their money situation.

Finding Your Strengths

If you lack confidence, the chances are that an antagonist will notice and take advantage of you. Have you ever noticed a newly planted tree that has been staked by a landscaper? You may think that the stakes will support the tree in the event of heavy winds. In most cases, newly planted trees don't need staking. It's often an unnecessary extra step that some landscapers perform. Unless the tree is super top-heavy, most newly planted trees do not need staking. Why?

Trees have a hormone called auxin, which helps play a vital role in the direction of a plant's growth. When you stake a tree, it can affect the caliper and taper of a tree's growth. Where am I going with this? I like to compare the growth of humans and trees because both share one thing—strength through adversity. I earned a horticulture degree after I retired from the Air Force and appreciate the symbiotic relationship we have with hard times and growing from them.

When the winds blow the trees around, the trees are busy producing auxin hormones to become stronger. As humans, you can also become confident if you look at your negative experiences and conquer them. Discern how you feel about yourself. Can we love ourselves more? Can we show ourselves more respect? Should we set healthier boundaries in our lives? We become more empowered when we understand the negative patterns in our lives that are repeating themselves over and over. We can all attract people in our lives that mistreat us or take advantage of us. It's up to us to reduce this kind of behavior.

Energy Begets Energy

Many scientists and others will tell you that everything is energy. Like energy attracts like energy. Pay attention to the thoughts in your head. Up to 90 percent of your belief system is in your subconscious. I learned this years ago when training to become a consulting hypnotist. Perhaps you were told you would not amount to anything in life because a parent was using reverse psychology to motivate you. You may have experienced being mocked or teased as a child.

Without realizing it, you may be attracting patterns of experiences you need to master for your growth. Yes, they can be very painful. No one wants mistreatment in their life. When you take responsibility to get the help you need, your life can change for the better. Behavior modification can help you feel more confident thus attracting fewer antagonists.

Learn More About Your Coworkers

People have more in common with other people than they may realize. It's part of our human nature to want to bond with people. Before you share too much information with a coworker or your supervisor, take time to learn if you can trust them. This investment will be worth it in the long run. People may hold power over you because you have shared something that they can use against you.

On the flip side, if you trust the person, by all means, let the other person know that you cried after watching a sad movie or you are grief-stricken because you lost a loved one. Trust your gut or your intuition when you are with another person. It always tells the truth. If you experience a traumatic experience from another person, mental health professionals are trained to deal with emotional grief and trauma. Be willing and open to receive help if you need it. Mental health professionals are trained to deal with emotional grief and trauma. Be willing and open to receive help. You may be surprised by what comes in your life to help you. I was shocked by an outcome that occurred in my life. I prayed many years ago for help to leave an abusive and alcoholic relationship. The experience I received was a huge surprise.

Sometimes Your Gift Comes in Ugly Wrapping Paper

I was in a long-term relationship with an alcoholic over twenty years ago. I went to an open Alcoholics Anonymous (AA) meeting for help and noticed everyone was so happy and smiling. But I felt broken and could not handle all the emotions in this small room. I ran out of the meeting room and ended up in a large cleaning closet in the building. Closing the closet door behind me, I was mortified and began crying.

First, I could not escape the happy people, and second, I was in a cleaning closet for crying out loud. I heard the message in my head: you belong in that meeting room, and I slowly walked back in that room for the moral support I needed. Everyone pretended they did not see me walking out of the cleaning closet. I realized I had a long way to go to help myself become healthier and whole again. I had become sicker than the alcoholic in my life and needed help.

My first husband, Michael, behaved like a narcissistic alcoholic who nearly strangled me in his blackouts. Our marriage vows of cherishing and protecting me were meaningless to him. I fought him off many times, and I knew he would kill me if I did not get help. He was strong, and it took all my energy to fight him off. We were both in denial. I was genuinely sick and grief-stricken, and it was affecting the quality of my life. Working twelve to fourteen hours a day was how I escaped from this madness and the ugliness in my personal life. I became a big overachiever in the Air Force and earned many prestigious awards. Does this sound familiar to you?

When the open AA meeting ended, one of the scruffiest men I had ever met in my life, asked me to follow him to his house to meet his wife. There was something about the man that made me trust him. I followed behind his old, beaten up car. Suspecting we were about to arrive at a trailer park, I mentally told myself it would be all right. Then we arrived at a multi-million-dollar home. I put my hands over my face in disgrace and embarrassment again. I had received another good lesson in one evening. Never judge a book by its cover. This man was not only incredibly wise—he was very wealthy too.

This beautiful beachfront home was the house I passed every day while out walking on the beach. I found solitude and grounding by breathing the salt air every day. The scruffy older man who came to my rescue was a retired Army helicopter pilot, and his wife was an accomplished author. Lessons! I tell you. When you ask for help, whether through praying or with intention, you will get what you need, but not always how you expect it.

I only had a few months with this man and this open AA group as I was about to move to a new state. I was open to helping myself, and it came most surprisingly. Be flexible in getting the help you deserve. Give yourself a gift-- take 100 percent accountability in becoming healthier and happier in your life. Trust the gut-feeling or scream inside your mind that you should walk away from a situation that will disempower you. Say no to narcissistic people and keep walking toward a more healthy and empowered life.

Write about who is mistreating you and how you feel about it. What's going on with your work issue? You can fill out this sheet or use a separate piece of paper.

An Extraordinary Woman Named Martha

Six years ago, I was hanging out with friends, and I overheard them talking about a wise woman named Martha. They were getting Reiki energy healing treatments from Martha. I was familiar with energy work. According to an online article by Collective Evolution, Quantum physicists discovered that physical atoms are made up of vortices of energy that are constantly spinning and vibrating. Matter, at its tiniest observable level, is energy, and human consciousness is connected to it, human consciousness can influence its behavior and even re-structure it.[1]

Well, I was naturally intrigued by all the laudatory comments about Martha. I asked how I could contact her and got her phone number. At that time, my stress levels were through the roof, and my health was severely declining because I was standing up to my workplace bullies and dealing with discrimination work matters. I remember the first day I went to visit her, and I could hardly put one foot in front of another. I was tired, weak, anxious, and depressed. I was also desperate to be in the company of a mature and compassionate person.

Martha was patient with me and knew I was a mental, physical, and spiritual wreck. I had been praying for a miracle, and what I received was unexpected. She was a retired nurse and not only understood the dynamics of a person's body, but she also knows how to bring out the best version of a person. She had seen the worst of me, heard my emotionally charged cry for help, and met me every step in supporting my health and well-being.

NOTE: *Who can support or mentor you to be more confident and courageous? It could be a clergy member, rabbi, priest, mental health professional, or a trained expert.*

Why Do You Care About What Others Think?

Liz Ryan, a seasoned Human Resources (HR) expert who writes for Huffington Post, *Business Week*, and other sources, states that The Social Contract was the deal our parents and grandparents took—the deal that said: "Stick with this company and work hard, and you'll get promoted and retire with a pension." That deal is long gone unless you work for the government.[2]

Most people will agree that times have changed in the workplace. You may feel that many employers are not loyal to employees, while managers may have the impression that many of their employees are not allegiant to the company. The American workforce culture has changed, and it affects everyone within its grasp. You cannot live in fear of upsetting your supervisor or manager. If you walk on eggshells for fear that you will upset your supervisor or manager, you are definitely in the wrong job. High evaluation ratings are nice, but you should have some career goals for yourself. You probably know your skill sets and what you are capable of doing.

The boss is probably going to tell you the company organization's goals at some point during your employment. However, it may not align with your goals and your vision. No one has to get trapped in other people's ideas or dreams. We all have the right to have our own dreams.

Write about the characteristics of a good supervisor or coworker. You can use this sheet, or you can use a separate sheet of paper. For example: Is your boss empathetic to your needs?

Personal Power

Here are three tips for finding your personal power and becoming more empowered in your life:

1 Part of being a human being is feeling valued, appreciated, and having a sense of belonging. No one on this earth is more valuable than you. Are you going so fast that you need to take yourself off of autopilot? Our society has conditioned us to go, go, go all the time, and often you are just busy and not as productive as you would like to be in your life. Slow down a little in your life and notice how much more peaceful you feel.

2 Stop worrying about what others will think of you. They are responsible for their thoughts and actions. If you ask twenty people how they would address a problem that involves you, you may get twenty different answers. Personal power is trusting yourself, allowing yourself to make mistakes, and learning from each opportunity. As my good friend Martha has always reminded me—we all see the same things, but we see them through different filters or lenses. You may meet people who "get" you and others who won't try to get to know you better.

3 If you are seeking answers or validation from everyone else but yourself, then please stop it right now! The answers are often within you. Stop asking someone else about how you should handle your affairs unless you are seeking professional advice. I see this over and over with people. They will ask me what I think about a matter involving them. I will turn it around in an empowering question and ask, "How are you giving away your personal power to me when you know better?"

Visualization Exercise

Close your eyes and think of a time when you felt courageous during a time of difficulty. Small victories count. Did you speak up for yourself? Did you take a step out of your comfort zone? Even if you felt uncomfortable—did you do something you felt was brave?

Write about your visualization—what images or thoughts came to your mind? Use this space or write on a separate piece of paper.

_____

_____

_____

_____

_____

_____

_____

_____

_____

_____

_____

_____

_____

_____

_____

_____

_____

_____

_____

_____

Courage Looks Great on You

I once attended an event for women, and the speakers touted makeup as the route to empowerment and success. If I had known this information ahead of time, I would not have attended. I passionately believe that looking good is essential to our self-esteem, but makeup comes off at the end of the day. We are imperfect human beings. We can rely on the trappings of makeup, undergarments that make us look better and beautiful clothes, but they only serve us for a while. Men usually don't get caught up in the marketing media madness that makes a women feel insecure and that she is not enough.

What is important is your thoughts, which form your belief system. How do you really feel inside? Are you making progress in your life? If you depend on your looks to get you where you want to go in life—you may be missing the mark and shortchanging yourself. It takes courage to live the life you want that is empowering.

The Power of Intention

Here are three powerful tips about how courage can move your forward. First, if you are working in a job where you are disrespected and not valued for your skill sets, it's time to evaluate your belief system. If you think that you can never find another job that will pay as much or offers the same benefits, you are mistaken. There are many jobs in the United States. that can be a better fit for you. If you are being mistreated in the workplace or feel uncomfortable in your job, that may push you to find a better job.

Often, your ego will tell you to play it safe. Listen to your intuition or gut feelings. You are on this earth for a reason and to share your gifts with others.

If you need to get more skills, go back to school, or take an evening course at your local college. Just don't settle for the status quo and feel you should be grateful to have the job you are in if it's unfulfilling or hostile. Know that you probably have many talents and skills that you have yet to use in the workforce. Tap into them and take action to find a better job.

Second, step up in your world and be 100 percent supportive to yourself. Maybe you want to work for yourself, or you have an idea that you would like to take further. It's OK to feel scared. There is no shame in being fearful. Feel the fear and move through it. Find a support team or a cheerleader who is on your side. Everyone feels fear at some time; you get to choose what side of fear you want to be on--the disempowered side or the empowered side.

For example, your family may try to persuade you to work in a job you hate, because they think it's a "safe" job. They may feel this way whether you are in a job they approve of or not. Empowerment means that you take the "reins" of your life and decide where you want to work or if you want to work for yourself. Hire a business start-up coach or go to an organization like SCORE (score.org). This organization gives free business advice from men and women who have run successful businesses and want to impart their knowledge to help others succeed as entrepreneurs. If you don't feel valued in your job, you may want to become an entrepreneur or you may want to be your own boss.

Third, whether you want to find a better job or become an entrepreneur, it takes money to pay your bills and to grow in business. If you don't have a savings account with enough money to fuel your dreams, it may be time to reconsider where you spend your money. You may have to cut back on purchasing fancy coffee, gym memberships, manicures, buying clothes, etc. When you conscientiously invest in yourself, you can move ahead in your life.

You will have naysayers in your life who will tell you how to live your life and tell you to be grateful for the miserable job. Ignore them or take their words with a grain of salt. Not everyone is going to understand why you left your old job or why you became an entrepreneur. The bottom line is that we are all entitled to live our lives fully and with great joy.

Educate Yourself on Work Policies and Laws

Some employees don't know the guidelines, laws, and protocols that support a healthy and respectful workplace environment. I remember a client named Theresa, who reached out to me about her managers placing false charges against her. She was afraid of retaliation because she turned in her managers for illegal actions. Here are three powerful tips:

1 If you know how to research your work's policies, guidelines, manuals, handbooks, etc., start studying how to help yourself. Perhaps you work for the city, state, or government; you can find the regulations or manuals online by searching for them. Often, there are disciplinary tables online for HR experts and managers to reference for taking disciplinary action towards an employee.

  You can share this information with an attorney or another professional. You may be able to use this as proof of discrimination or retaliation, especially if you have filed charges against your workplace with the Office of Special

Counsel, Equal Employment Opportunity Commission, or another federal agency.

2 If you don't have the time or the energy to do your research on regulations, etc., consider an employment or labor attorney. You may have to pay for their legal service, but if economically challenged, you may qualify for pro bono service. The Resources chapter will provide you with information on legal services.

3 When you deal with antagonists, they may be desperate to defame you, fire you, or ruin your credibility. It does not matter how strong you think you are; everyone has a breaking point, and bullies will do their best to find the weak link in your defenses. It can take a severe toll on your health. It's important to find avenues of relaxation that resonate with you. I will cover this later in the workbook.

Do your best to focus on everything good in your life. When your mind wanders on any negativity, be sure to bring it back to neutral or a more positive thought. Our thoughts form our belief system. You are worthy of claiming your personal power and having a healthy work environment. You will likely grow the most when you are out of your comfort zone and take healthy risks in your life. Find a reputable mental health practitioner or a certified life coach who specializes in "personal power."

Reach out to a long-standing coaching organization that can refer you to certified coaches. One of my favorite organizations is the Institute for Professional Excellence in Coaching (iPEC). I attended their training in 2013 and highly recommend their program. I have listed their contact information in the Resources section.

Write about the best thing you can be doing for yourself at this time. For example, seeking a mental health care practitioner for support or hiring an employment attorney for legal advice. You can use this space or a separate piece of paper.

#HateNoOne

There is no room for hatred. We were not born hating anyone. Those who discriminate and mistreat others learned it somewhere in their life. You can support yourself and learn how to outmaneuver workplace bullying and discrimination. Once you have been able to stand up for yourself, you realize that you can do this in all areas of your life.

While you may not want the role of an advocate for others in your workplace suffering from bullying and discrimination, you can still help others by sharing the tips and advice from this book It's in helping others that you will likely heal your own life. I know, because for every person I have ever supported, I have felt divine healing in my own life. I have come to realize that other people may have to go through their journey of abuse and many other traumatic occurrences to learn from their experiences.

Even when I had those weeks where I had only ten dollars in my bank account, and I had to decide whether to eat or to put gas in my truck, I was still grateful to have ten dollars. At that time, the Veteran Affairs had turned off my paycheck, and I struggled financially. I never missed a meal, and I have never regretted my choice to stand up to workplace bullying and discrimination.

Sometimes another person may believe in you before you may believe in yourself. Remember that life is full of learning opportunities. Learn them wisely and do your best not to repeat mistakes that you can avoid. There will be days when you feel down, and you feel the world is against you. Take heart; process the feelings you are experiencing and remember that you get to look at life anyway you choose.

Give yourself a pat on the back or some praise for any accomplishments (personal or work) you have made at this time—all accomplishments count! Write about your achievements. For example, did you sell things you no longer needed and build up your savings account? You can use this space or a separate piece of paper.

CHAPTER TWO

Bullying in the Workplace

This chapter discusses:

- Definition of bullying
- Does mediation work for clashing parties?
- Examples of workplace bullying
- Workplace bullying is not illegal, but you can still support yourself
- Persona of a bully
- Workplace bullying insights
- Should you go to HR if you are experiencing bullying or discrimination?

Definition of Bullying

You may wonder what workplace bullying is, and my definition is when another person(s) mistreats, harms, or abuses you in the workplace. Bullying can occur on a mental or physical level. Sadly, it is not illegal in the United States at the time of writing this workbook. If you are experiencing bullying in the workplace, take heart.

Everyone has different coping strategies and tools. Some people get stressed very quickly, and others can handle more stress in their lives. While some of the strategies and guidance in this book may seem easy, there are parts in this workbook that may make you uncomfortable. Please be gentle and kind to yourself. It may take a while before you can move to the next step or strategy, but remember, every step forward is towards being more empowered.

Does mediation work if I am having a work issue?

Some companies offer mediation if a work issue arises. Mediation offers an intervention between clashing parties to promote a compromise, settlement, or some kind of reconciliation. A trained (neutral) mediator is often brought in to facilitate the session. If both parties can reach an agreement, that decision or action will settle the issue. This can save time and money for all parties as a faster way to resolve workplace conflicts. I perform mediations in my hometown of Asheville, North Carolina. I have seen the power of mediation when two angry people come together and leave with a mutual decision that supports each person. Agreements can sometimes be accomplished in a two-hour session.

On the other hand, if the workplace issue is a serious matter such as blatant discrimination, you may want to address it with the Equal Employment Opportunity Commission (EEOC.gov) or another federal agency. Often, bullying feels like discrimination, but while bullying is not illegal in the workforce, discrimination is illegal according to the EEOC. I will address discrimination later in this workbook.

Examples of Workplace Bullying

1. Workers or managers ignore you. You may be isolated because the bullies want to exclude you from meetings, parties, or other social gatherings. Sometimes it is made clear that the bullies don't want you around.
2. You suffer verbal lashings or abuse at work by peers, supervisors, or managers. Coworkers or supervisors criticize you in private or public about your work performance. The point may be to slander you, and even you may question your worth to this organization.
3. Coworkers or supervisors gang up on you at work. You do not feel valued or appreciated in the workplace.
4. Your wellbeing is declining, and you are having concerns about your mental and physical health. You may be seeing a medical professional for health issues that are appearing in your life.
5. Supervisors ignore your project or task while someone else receives the praise you deserve, publicly. Perhaps your evaluations are downgraded even though you are exceeding your goals.
6. You have been given more work than your coworkers and asked to perform these tasks beyond the set work standards.
7. Your peers, supervisor, or managers may stare at you, making you feel uncomfortable and even stalked. They may also get quiet when you walk near them.
8. You realize there may be an agenda to remove you from your job. There may be an overt or underhanded, sneaky campaign to run you out of the company.

Exercise: Workplace Bullying Checklist

Are you experiencing bullying? Place a check by each statement that describes or is similar to your experience in the workplace.

☐ 1. Workers or managers isolate you and don't want you in the workplace.

☐ 2. You suffer verbal lashings or abuse at work by peers, supervisors, or managers. You receive criticism for your performance in private or public.

☐ 3. You feel ganged up on at work. You are not feeling valued or appreciated in the workplace.

☐ 4. Your wellbeing is declining, and you are concerned about your mental and physical health.

☐ 5. Supervisors ignore you because someone stole your idea or project.

☐ 6. You have been given more work than your coworkers and asked to perform these tasks beyond the set standards. Perhaps someone has sabotaged your work to make you look irresponsible.

☐ 7. Your peers, supervisors, or managers may be watching you constantly, making you feel uncomfortable and even stalked.

☐ 8. You suspect there is a plan to remove you from your job.

☐ 9. You receive downgraded evaluations even though you are exceeding your goals.

☐ 10. Your coworkers are receiving recognition or awards, but not you.

If you checked even one of these statements, it's an opportunity to stand up to bullying in the workplace. If you checked one or two, you may experience bullying. If you scored three to five on this checklist, you are definitely being bullied. Last, if you have checked off more than five on this checklist, you are experiencing "extreme bullying."

NOTE: *These are some examples of workplace bullying, and there may be additional instances. Bullying is different from discrimination in the workplace. Discrimination will be discussed later in this workbook.*

Whistleblowers Take High Risks

I have never met a Whistleblower who did not pay a high price for exposing illegal activities or prohibited personnel actions of a company. The Free Dictionary defines a Whistleblower as one who reveals wrongdoings within an organization to the public or to those in a position of authority.[3]

I interviewed Erin Brockovich on my podcast, *The Empowered Whistleblower*, in April 2018. She addressed the fact that whistleblowing receives a bad name, but it should not, as everyone knows right from wrong. Since I was a whistleblower myself and experienced extreme bullying for speaking out against wrongful activities in my previous job, I know the ugly tactics an antagonist will use to try to run you off, defame you, or even break you.

You can be mistreated for speaking out against your company, agency, or organization for unlawful activities. The people you report may abuse you. When people speak out against dangerous situations or illegal actions, they face emotional, reputational, and social risks. Whistleblowers can become the target of revenge, spite, or betrayal, along with other negative behavior from others in the workplace.

If you believe you need to speak up about illegal or prohibited personnel practices in your company, be sure you have a reliable support team. You may need spiritual/religious staff, legal experts, HR consultants, and other professionals who can advise you and be there if you are experiencing harassment for reporting fraud, illegal activities, etc. Some people think they are stronger than the bullies. These people believe they can endure the harassment, but long-term bullying can affect your health and wellbeing. Everyone has a breaking point of what they can endure with harassment.

A client of mine, Phillip, told me he spent years in the military and that he felt he could not be "broken" by his bullies. Within four months, he contacted me in tears because his coworkers mocked him at work. Bullying can be very sneaky. Phillip's supervisors harassed him after he reported illegal activities and was in a "protected status with the Office of Special Counsel (OSC)." He had filed allegations that were being processed and reviewed by OSC's staff. Phillip was able to show proof of retaliation to his case manager, and fortunately, he was offered a settlement for the harassment by his company.

Thankfully, more people have become appreciative of those who have the courage, strength, and tenacity to hold people who act badly accountable. Positive change can only occur when people step up and report personnel who are unethical. I am so grateful to all the courageous men and women out there who make our world a better place. They hold a special place in my heart.

I wrote an article, "Spending a Morning with Erin Brockovich," for the Good Men Project. I shared how two women wanted change in their community of Hannibal, Missouri and called in Brockovich. The city may sound familiar—author Mark Twain was born in Hannibal. Twain wrote many novels and short stories including *Huckleberry Finn* and was world-famous. Erin Brockovich went to Hannibal to educate the community on why there was lead in their water system. The lead in their water was higher than some of Flint, Michigan's lead levels.

The two Hannibal women ran for their city council and won. Positive change can happen in the community. The women immediately set out to change how their water was regulated and no more ammonia was allowed in the water. Thanks to these two persistent women, the town had clean and safe water. All of us can make simple changes, which positively impact everyone.[4]

The Risks of Firing Federal Employees Too Quickly

Most of my federal clients have experienced retaliation for filing complaints against their managers or coworkers. They received terrible appraisals or evaluations after they spoke up about discrimination or bullying matters in the workplace. In each case, they had received outstanding evaluations in the past, and they had received awards for being a stellar employee. Federal employees can be fired faster than years ago.

In May of 2018, President Trump passed an Executive Order in which federal employees could be removed sooner for poor work performance. As a seasoned HR expert, I know it's the right thing to remove someone capable but not meeting their assigned work standards. I wrote an excerpt for an article for the Good Men Project as a columnist. "There is another side to how removing federal employees may negatively impact not only the employee but every one of us who depend on federal agencies to fulfill their mission fairly and responsibly. What about those courageous (whistleblowing) federal employees who speak out against illegal, prohibited personnel practices, fraud, and other matters that ultimately impact every one of us that our government serves?"

Yes, we are all affected by the deeds and actions of every federal employee. Do we want to see an honest "whistleblower" fired from the federal government for speaking up about something dishonest? If an agency is not fulfilling its mission ethically, it trickles down to every individual impacted by the acts of dishonesty. I have witnessed federal employees speaking up about nepotism, discrimination, and prohibited personnel practices. Later, their supervisors placed them on a Performance Improvement Plan (PIP), with the intent to remove that person from their federal job. This action is one of the fastest ways to remove a federal employee, whether they deserve to be removed from their position or not.

As of 2018, there have been changes in federal PIPs. The executive order specifically standardizes the length of an employee performance improvement plan (PIP) to thirty days. In the past, some agencies gave their employees anywhere from thirty to 120 days to demonstrate their level of performance.[5] If the federal employee does not meet the performance standards after additional training, it can be grounds to remove the employee. A quick way to unfairly get rid of a whistleblower is to put them on a PIP, unless they merit being put on a PIP.[6] If you want to report your workplace for illegal activities, make sure you have a "team" of people who can support you. For example, you may want to consult with an attorney who handles whistleblower cases.

Bullying in the Workplace

There are numerous reasons why employees experience bullying in the workplace. You may be dealing with a narcissist or psychopath in your workplace. The most significant personal growth often requires you to step outside of your comfort zone. It's extraordinarily difficult for some people to speak up for themselves, talk to their HR department about being mistreated, and set healthy boundaries in their lives.

Should I go to the media if I am mistreated in the workplace?

A few of my clients have asked me if they should reach out to the media and expose their antagonists. Most of the news we hear and listen to is full of "sensationalism." Your story could make the local or the national news. Alan shared a video of being mistreated in the workplace that ended up on the news. Thankfully, he had a good outcome after embarrassing his company. Exposing your antagonist on media has its pros and cons.

My advice is if you want to reach out to the media, be sure you have evidence to support your claim of mistreatment. Also, consider if you can remain an employee at your company. You may face some backlash or get fired. It's always best to think ahead and have a solid plan for your "tomorrow." Consider if you have enough money in the bank to support yourself and if you can handle angry people in your company. Is it worth going to the media or taking an alternative route? Think about the consequences and if it's worth it to go to the media.

The Ultimate Question ... Should You Go to HR for Help?

It's normal to feel uncomfortable going to your HR department for help. I tell my clients it's up to you to make that decision. Personally, I like a documentation trail to show I went to HR for assistance. You may need that later on if you experience backlash or not being supported by HR. I will get into documenting "HR communication" later in this workbook. The HR department may be part of your management when it comes to your work hierarchy. If you have an HR department where you work, it may be an internal work obligation to seek an HR expert's assistance in dealing with discrimination or bullying. *But*—are they there to support you in your time of need? I am going to share some information to enlighten you.

Five insights on seeking HR's assistance with your matter.

1 You must understand that the HR representative is often part of the management. They are usually required to keep the company leadership apprised of any problems in the workplace. Your leadership will likely want to know if there is dissension in their work environment.

   If your agency is in the civilian sector, the cost, time, and energy spent on Equal Employment Opportunity (EEO) matters or other agencies could destroy or cost the company much embarrassment. Settlement fees or court costs will likely come out of the company owner's pocket. If it's a government agency, there are still issues of money, embarrassment, and time spent on litigation, but settlement comes from the federal agency.

2 An HR expert in your workplace may purposely try to downplay your accusations of discrimination or bullying because they know how serious the matter can be if it becomes an EEO claim or more. HR may turn it around on you and make comments that make you fear you may lose your job over your concerns. However, be sure you still work with your HR department in order to show that you addressed your matter. Turn around and send a clarification email to HR and share what you understood took place at the meeting.

Always print that email out and hand carry it to a safe place. Never keep it at work. I will share how to document an email trail to HR, later in this workbook.

3 Instead of relying on HR to be your subject matter expert (SME), learn everything you can about your rights at your workplace. You can research policies and laws that would apply in your case. The internet is a great tool for access to work policies, statutes, and more. If this is not for you—consider hiring a professional expert to help you with your matter. If lack of money is an issue, you may qualify for pro bono assistance from an attorney. Check out the resources section in the back of this workbook for more information.

4 If you file charges against your company or agency, you may face retaliation that can come in many forms. It is possible, and it does happen, that some HR folks will keep people in the dark about their workplace rights in order to support the management. HR may later be involved in attempts to fire you, discredit you, or slander you. Bullying is not illegal; however, discrimination and retaliation are unlawful, according to the Equal Employment Opportunity Commission (EEOC).

5 I want to wrap this up by reminding you that there are many good HR employees out there and many who care about your circumstances. You may never know if they genuinely want to help you but for whatever reason, they don't give you the support you need and deserve. You can still move forward to another person for help or reach out to the EEOC for more help. You can always take other actions, and you can use the email documentation that you reached out to your HR personnel for assistance. This information can come in handy when seeking legal support, unemployment compensation, and pursuing litigation on your matter.[7]

CHAPTER THREE

The Persona of a Bully

This chapter discusses:

- The makeup of a bully
- Narcissistic bullies and other types of bullies
- The high cost of bullying

The Makeup of a Bully or an Antagonist

Bullies are not made up of sugar and spice. They have created so much harm in my life and probably, yours too. I have learned a lot about their behavior and how to stay strong if you are affected by a workplace antagonist. It's tough to accept that other people can misbehave and hurt others, but it's becoming an epidemic issue in the American workplace.

Understanding why the antagonist harasses people is vital so that you can work through your matters of bullying. It's essential to know the persona of an antagonist. Author Anton Hout's examples of workplace bullies on his website (www.overcomebullying.org) inspired me. Here are some bully personalities you might recognize.

Two-Faced Liar: They smile and try to be friendly while trying to get you to trust them but later lie about statements or actions that are not yours. They thrive on the game of deceit and manipulation.

Obnoxious Intimidator: This person is loud and unruly when they want to prove their point or get the attention they seek. You may witness this kind of bully yelling at managers or other employees. They try to control others with their wrath and abhorrent behavior. They are often successful in their attempts to dominate others.

Narcissistic Antagonist: This is the person who enjoys hurting and scaring you. They love dominating you and coercing you to behave in a certain way. This bully could care less about your self-esteem, safety, or well-being. They delight in the harm they inflict on you. They may also be very charming, while underneath, they are waiting for the right time to attack you.

Persecuting Competitor: This may be your co-worker or another employee who knows you are more competent than they are in the workplace. They may try to form alliances with management and complain about you and your work to elevate their status. Generally, they feel insecure especially when they compare themselves to you or other coworkers. This kind of bully can wreak much havoc in the workplace when they are against you.

Territory Protector: This bully is very territorial. For example, they may have inside trade knowledge, but they will never share it with you. They may be more skilled or knowledgeable from years of working in a company, but they will not relinquish knowledge that will help others with their work or help coworkers get promoted. This person is in it only for themselves.

Office Bully: Some companies have this type of bully. They are the ones who always put others down; they look for flaws or weaknesses in others and expose them. The Office Bully may even sabotage your work to make you look bad. They love making others look ineffective and incompetent.

I Am in Charge Bully: When a supervisor is in charge and has an ego larger than life, they may mistreat their subordinates. For example, they give them harder work assignments, make them work more extended hours than other employees, or humiliate this person so that they are afraid they may lose their job if they don't bow down. In my experience, I've noticed that unfortunately quite a few employees work for a bully like this type.

According to an online article in *Psychology Today*, "Bullies are notorious for misusing power. They may overtly denigrate, criticize, or exclude you in such a way that, at the time, you may be incapable of responding. In a group meeting, they may covertly destroy you by responding to a comment or suggestion you make with a remark alluding to the idea that they don't understand what you are talking about—suggesting that you are inarticulate or ignorant—and not allow for clarification."

But even more insidious is an antagonist's capacity to manipulate or incite others to be aggressive, belittling, or hostile toward you through their denigrating remarks or creation of rumors. The farther they push you down, the more they rise to the top. And they do succeed.[8]

The article states that personality disorders are complex, and bully characteristics may not belong to one diagnosis. Some antagonists want to protect their shame and anxieties about their failures or shortcomings. The bullies like to take attention away from themselves and denigrate their targets, which makes the bullied experience anxiety and humiliation. The focus is on the person who received bullying.

Self-Esteem

Although it is a popularly held belief that bullies suffer from low self-esteem and are acting out to compensate, some research suggests that these individuals have high self-esteem. However, bullies have pathologically high self-esteem that is also unstable (Baumeister, 2001).[9]

This article further states that when an antagonist is feeling emotionally or psychologically insulted in any way, this is an ego threat that provokes extreme negative feelings the bully cannot tolerate. In turn, the antagonist lashes out defensively in anger to defend their individual image that they are powerful, in control, and superior to others. According to the University at Buffalo School of Management, more than 475,000 participants in a three-decade span revealed that men are more likely than women to be narcissistic.

Men are also more likely to exploit others and feel entitled to certain privileges than women. Regarding assertiveness and desire for power, men took the lead in these categories too. Targets of antagonists often think that they have little or no control in the workplace. I will later share how you do have control over your belief system and strategies on how to command more respect from others.

The American Psychiatric Association: Diagnostic and Statistical Manual of Mental Disorders offers insights to a myriad of mental disorders. You can purchase the book to learn more about this subject, but it's not really necessary. No one should ever mistreat you, even if they have a mental disorder.

Narcissism

When I typed narcissism in my computer search engine, about 31,500,000 results showed up. Do you think this is a hot topic and it's important? I think it's a critical subject and especially in the workplace. In "14 Signs you're Dealing with a Narcissist," an article by Dr. Margalis Fjelstad, she states that as far as superiority and entitlement goes, "The world of the narcissist is all about good/bad, superior/inferior, and right/wrong. There is a definite hierarchy, with the narcissist at the top—which is the only place he feels safe. Narcissists have to be the best, the most right, and the most competent; do everything their way; own everything, and control everyone."[10]

I appreciate how she further breaks down narcissistic traits, where narcissist people want lots of attention and validation. People with these traits have an extremely high need for everything in their life to be perfect. Narcissists always want to be in control, blame others if things don't go their way, have a lack of boundaries and empathy, are unreasonable, split things into good and bad parts, and have lives full of fear and anxiety. She shares that narcissists don't feel shame, and they cannot empathize with others and work as a team.

Is this kind of person working at your job? Possibly. When you spot someone, who exhibits these kinds of character traits, you may want to protect yourself from that person. You will never be able to change this person by being kind to them. Don't get sucked into thinking that you have to be abused by this kind of person—you don't. It's always best to be civil with everyone at work. You never know if your actions can be used against you if you are uncivil with anyone at your job. You may have to leave your job and find a better suited position or look at honing your skills to work for yourself. You have the power to make choices in your life that will empower you.

Antagonists may come into your life. You can support yourself in standing up to them, finding self-love, self-respect, and more. It's up to you to master each lesson and to find peace in your heart. You may be thinking that a particular person is driving you crazy with their behavior or comments. Narcissistic bullies love to create misery in your life.

Narcissistic Deanna

Don't give away your personal power. I suggest you smile at your bully and walk away peacefully if you can. You can experience trauma from interacting with a narcissist. Seek professional care with a mental health practitioner or an expert in trauma if needed. Be sure to check out the resources section at the back of this workbook.

My best teacher was a narcissistic antagonist, and she knew how to upset me, like no other person on this earth. I learned from my mentor to be kind to her and to visualize loving and white energy around her. While I love my mentor, I thought it would be a cold day in Hell before I could be kind to someone who abused people and often got away with it. Well, I gave it a shot. Deanna would always walk in on me, while I was talking to someone, and act like I did not exist. In the past, she won when I got mad. The reaction of me becoming angry was her highest goal. One day, I did follow my mentor's advice, and when Deanna interrupted my conversation with the intent of upsetting me, I stopped and smiled at her. Her face began to match her frizzy red hair.

I kept talking to her and asked how her day was going. She was so mad at me having mastery of myself that she was speechless for about twenty seconds and stormed out of the room. I have to admit, I have an incredible mentor, and her advice worked in my situation. After that, the woman stayed pretty far from me. She realized that I had claimed my personal power, and she had no mastery over me any longer. I wished I had learned the lesson sooner, but life is a journey of education by great teachers. If you are wondering if being kind to the narcissistic woman was hard, I admit it was difficult at first, but extremely rewarding in the end.

It may take a professional mental health expert to support you in recovery. If someone emotionally upsets you or their actions trigger you, there could be some unsolved or unhealed issues in your life. Bullying may trigger you, and a mental health professional may assist you in supporting your recovery.

A Life Coach or mentor who facilitates empowering clients may support you in having a breakthrough about why you are attracting people who mistreat you. You may find a spiritual or religious mentor who helps you to become a better version of yourself. It's generally easier to experience peace and happiness when you have a mentor or expert you trust and respect. They can hold you accountable for your personal growth. When you work on your personal growth, it may be uncomfortable, but there is nothing like owning your story, instead of your story owning you.

Because narcissists are in the work culture, you may need to find a more suitable job if you are dealing with this kind of person. You can't change them, but you can change your circumstances. There are all kinds of support in your community or within reach. I strongly suggest you protect yourself and make a decision that empowers you. It's not worth the harm that is inflicting you in a position where you must suffer daily.

In some cases, workplaces can become so dangerous and toxic that it creates a hostile and unsafe culture. Unfortunately, workplace violence is on the rise. Stories of active shooters and workplace violence are making national headlines. It's important to know what you can do about it. Felix Nater, a highly sought out security consultant, states, "Workplace violence prevention is an ongoing process involving multiple intervention strategies of which leadership and training supports the policy, plans, procedures, and security. Creating a safe workplace, employers have an ethical, moral, legal, and financial duty to provide a safe workplace. However, employees have a comparable duty and obligation to bring potentially violent situations to the school or employer's attention."

Standing up to bullying is not for everyone, and never feel bad if you trust your gut and walk away from a lousy job or situation. Never feel you are weak for not choosing the path of confrontation. That is very disempowering and doesn't acknowledge that you are capable of owning your personal power and creating healthy choices in your life. Honor your gut feelings or your intuition when you get insights into knowledge. I will discuss setting healthy boundaries and how to stand up for yourself later in this book.

Felix Nater further states, "It's important to remember that when setting boundaries, you consider the adverse impact of the emotional spontaneous reaction. You must remember that once you violate either the workplace rules or your personal boundaries the consequences will only complicate the situation. If you decide to retaliate out of frustration, you may expose yourself to the employer's Workplace Violence Zero Tolerance Policy. Remember, as difficult as it may seem at the time, I recommend walking away and documenting the experience."

Bullying in the workplace is a dangerous cycle and costs millions of dollars in medical and psychological care. Many targets of bullying want stricter laws to stop bullying in the workplace, or to ensure there are more stringent laws for disciplining bullies. Most people don't realize that there are laws that protect employees in the United States. Often, by the time the target gets to their hearing or court date, the antagonists may have created so much damage to that person that they will often throw in the towel or settle for less than they deserve.

There are many resources you can reach out to for advice on workplace bullying, but make sure they are credible resources. If you suffer from low self-esteem or have a hard time loving yourself, you can become your own biggest antagonist and punish yourself, instead of nurturing yourself. Felix Nater shares "that whether you are a victim of a bully supervisor or coworker, you lose control when you lose self-control and emotionally cross the line of civility. The bully wants you to fall for the bait so that they can manage you in their territory."

They want the emotional outburst to emphasize you as the problem. So, do not fall for the bait. Manage your self-esteem and if you know you can't try to avoid being baited into a confrontation of any kind. There may be some horrific events that have happened in your past, and you still carry these stories in your head. It's time to become your own best friend and love the person you see in the mirror recognizing that self-control is your best friend. Individuals who reflect respect for themselves tend to experience less workplace bullying than employees who project low self-esteem.

The individual who projects the low self-esteem wears a bulls-eye on their chest that attracts others. Low self-esteem lowers your confidence in managing your boundaries and managing your behaviors. While I do not want you to be aggressive, a little bit of assertiveness will project self-confidence.

The most exceptional opportunity of all is to learn from all your experiences and move forward as a happier and more empowered individual. One of my favorite authors, Brene Brown, says, "If we don't share our stories, we can't fully heal." I find it very healing to share what we have learned on this journey we call life.

NOTE: *Be sure to document any bullying, even if you aren't willing to report it. You may need this information later. You can also reach out to your Union for support if you have one. Remember, you don't deserve to be treated badly in the workplace. Don't let it consume your thoughts. You can send an email to the antagonist and tell them to stop harassing you. Last, consider reporting the bullying incident to your managers. They need to know about workplace issues where people are being mistreated. I will cover email communication and samples in the documentation chapter.*

Write about an outcome that helped support you. Did you seek professional care or help? How did you manage the situation? For example, someone may have offered to mentor you. Use this space or a separate piece of paper.

CHAPTER FOUR

Statistics and Guidance on Workplace Bullying and Discrimination

This chapter discusses:

- Bullying highlights
- EEOC posters
- The bystander effect
- IRS guidelines on settlements
- Slander and libel
- Social Media "dos" and "don'ts"
- Phone tapping
- Financial fitness

Depending on where you look for statistics on workplace bullying, you will get a varying degree of evidence. One thing I know for sure is that many people experience workplace bullying. Bystanders rarely step in to support the bullied employee for fear of retaliation. Employees who promise to be a witness for an employee may get scared and feel they can't keep their promise. We are living in an epidemic of incivility, harassment, and discrimination in the workforce.

Here are some workplace bullying insights:

- Unfortunately, most employers and coworkers will do nothing to aid a bullied coworker.
- Less than 20 percent of employers will help a bullied target.
- Coworkers rarely assist the targets of bullying
- Most bullying targets are kind, cooperative, and agreeable people per many statistics on workplace bullying.[11]

The Startling Statistics

- 65.6 million people are affected by bullying, including targets and witnesses.
- 69 percent of workplace bullies are men, while 60 percent of bullying targets

are women.

- Targets lose their jobs at a significantly higher rate than antagonists (82 percent vs. 18 percent).
- 61 percent of all targets of bullying end up losing their jobs.
- In 2011, half of the employees in one survey said they were treated rudely at least once a week, an increase of 25 percent from 1998.
- Many workplace bullies also score high on tests of narcissism and self-orientation.
- Currently, federal law doesn't prohibit workplace bullying, but individual states are pushing to change that.[12]
- According to a poll by Weber Shandwick, 65 percent of Americans say the lack of civility is a major problem in the country and feel the negative tenor has worsened during the financial crisis and recession.[13]
- During the fiscal year 2015, EEOC received approximately 28,000 charges from employees alleging harassment while working for private employers or state and local government.

EEOC Posters Must Be Visible at Work

The law requires an employer to post notices describing the federal laws prohibiting job discrimination based on race, color, sex, national origin, religion, age, equal pay, disability, and genetic information. EEOC's poster is available in English, Arabic, Chinese, and Spanish. You can download or read online information about age, disability, pregnancy, race/color, religion, and other valuable information on the EEOC's website.[14]

Some employment practices could filter out individuals with minimum height requirements, citizenship requirements, or policies against hiring individuals with a prior conviction or arrest records. Minimum height requirements may be required to perform work duties safely and efficiently, but it could negatively affect Asians or Hispanics. Another employment policy that can determine employment is a high school diploma requirement, which may not be job-related for certain jobs such as laborers.[15]

What Is the Bystander Effect?

The bystander effect occurs when the presence of others discourages an individual from intervening in an emergency situation. Social psychologists Bibb Latané and John Darley popularized the concept following the infamous 1964 Kitty Genovese murder in New York City. Genovese was stabbed to death outside her apartment, while bystanders who observed the crime never assisted or called the police.

Latané and Darley attributed the bystander effect to the perceived diffusion of responsibility (onlookers are more likely to intervene if there are few or no other witnesses) and social influence (individuals in a group monitor the behavior of those around them to determine how to act). In the Genovese case, each onlooker concluded from their neighbors' inaction that their own personal help was not needed.[16]

Emotional Distress or Mental Anguish

Let's jump ahead—if you receive a settlement from filing a grievance, you may be required to report it on your annual taxes. The IRS has guidelines on what must be reported on your taxes. You may not have to claim your settlement as wages, according to the IRS.

According to the Internal Revenue Service (IRS)... The proceeds you receive for emotional distress or mental anguish originating from a personal physical injury or physical sickness are treated the same as proceeds received for personal physical injuries or physical sickness above.

But... If the proceeds you receive for emotional distress or mental anguish do not originate from a personal physical injury or physical sickness, you must include them in your income. However, the amount you must include is reduced by (1) amounts paid for medical expenses attributable to emotional distress or mental anguish not previously deducted and (2) previously deducted medical expenses for such distress and anguish that did not provide a tax benefit.

Attach to your return a statement showing the entire settlement amount less related medical costs not previously deducted and medical costs deducted for which there was no tax benefit. The net taxable amount should be reported as Other Income on line 21 of Form 1040.[17] You can always contact the IRS on whether or not you have to claim your settlement as wages.

Dos and Don'ts on Social Media

Sharing your concerns or your victories on social media can feel great. It can feel gratifying to get approval or likes on your posts. But can your social media posts backfire on you? Yes, they can. If you are venting about your workplace bullying and using a person's name, you could be committing defamation of character. Even if the statements are correct, be ready to defend your statements with evidence. If you are not sure about what you can discuss or write about regarding your bullying or discrimination matter, contact an employment attorney for guidance. Be safe, and don't get yourself in trouble.

When I was in the "discovery" phase of my EEO process, I provided documentation evidence to the defendant's attorney. These documents provided evidence in the EEO formal hearing process. I provided all the documentation evidence that would be used by the defendant's attorney. I was a little surprised that the VA attorney provided thirty pages of my Facebook social media as evidence. Still, I was not worried, as I have never written any type of offensive or libelous comments against my former agency. You never know who may be reading it, and it's not how I communicate on social media. My guess is that the VA attorney wanted to prove to me they could access my Facebook posts to rattle me.

Social Media

If you join a Facebook group, be careful what you post. Keep out names and circumstances around your workplace issues that could be used against you if it falls into the wrong hands. There are cases where the antagonist or their attorney has compiled social media posts against the bullied. If you have made social media posts that could be potentially damaging to you if they fall into the right hands, do your best to delete those posts right away. There is no way a Facebook administrator, who is in charge of a workplace bullying support group, will know who the antagonist is in their Facebook groups unless they know them personally.

Anyone can request to join a social media group. Always be careful what you post on social media. If you have a court hearing or an Equal Employment Opportunity Community (EEOC) hearing, the antagonist or attorneys representing the antagonist may attempt to find a way to access your social media. They may look for social media posts that contain defamation or negativity that could help them leverage control over you. For example, if you are pursuing an EEO hearing, you have signed a statement that you cannot discuss your case, except with certain professionals. Your case can be thrown out by the EEOC because you discussed your case with others that don't fall under the EEOC criteria.

Don't beat yourself up if you have made defamatory remarks about an antagonist. Just be mindful in the future and protect yourself. You never want an antagonist to hold power over you, especially if you can prevent it. Reach out to resources that can help or encourage you. Be mindful of social media groups or any group individuals that focus only on the negativity of their situation. Everyone's story is compelling to them.

Be cautious and mindful of each person's contribution to the group. Are they positive or negative? It is very cathartic to share how you feel about your bullying situation. Most people want to become empowered and want to know how to stand up to workplace bullying. Pay attention to the people you surround yourself with online and offline because their energy will rub off on you. There is a saying, "pay attention to the five people you hang around most of the time."

Write about how you are feeling at this time. What would you like to write about without any inhibition? For example, are you feeling more educated, empowered or are you feeling overwhelmed with your work issue? Use this space to write or feel free to use a separate piece of paper.

....

....

....

....

....

....

....

....

....

....

Phone Tapping

It may be hard to believe that someone would tap into your phone to listen to your conversation, but it does happen. Some of my clients wrote to their phone companies and requested to know if their personal home phone or cell phone was being "monitored" by someone other than themselves. Some of my clients had an attorney write to their cell phone companies or whoever managed their landlines and requested information on "phone monitoring" regarding their clients.

Sure enough, "warrants" were issued to monitor some of my clients' cell phones. Those "federal" warrants were handed over to their employment attorneys and were addressed during the court proceedings. I can't imagine anyone thinking it's fair for someone who filed for any kind of harassment charges, to have their phone monitored; it's not only wrong, but it violates a person's privacy.

Loss of Income or Finances

How financially fit are you if you lose your job or leave a bad job? Being broke can be a serious problem. Many people feel a sense of security if they have money in the bank and can live a particular lifestyle. You never want to experience a financial disaster. For the sake of feeling more confident, let's look at how you can raise money, so you have savings in the bank if you are fired from your job or choose to leave a toxic workplace.

Being Broke and Still Surviving

One of the most fearful situations for a person can be being fired and going broke. This happened to me—the broke part. My management placed me on administrative leave for about 100 days. After that, I was in an unpaid status until I settled with my former agency. I struggled to pay my attorney fees and pay for an expensive house. I survived, but I had to sell my beautiful home and give up many nice things to survive on a lot less money. I went through my savings at lightning speed. I can sincerely state that you learn to be creative when you have little money. I also learned it was not the end of the world, and you can restore your credit scores if needed. I sold many of the things I had collected over the years, and the more stuff I got rid of, the more liberated I felt.

Your earnings or your possessions may never make you feel secure; it must come from within yourself. Living a simpler life taught me to slow down and to take better care of myself. Funny how adversity can bring out the best version of yourself—if you let it. If you lose your job or you have a lot less money, try not to despair. There are some great programs out there like United Way's 2-1-1 program (www.211.org) that can likely help you.

Here are some resources they offer:
- Supplemental food and nutrition programs
- Shelter and housing options and utility assistance
- Employment and education opportunities
- Services for veterans
- Healthcare
- Addiction prevention and rehabilitation programs
- Support groups for individuals with mental illnesses or special needs

You can contact this program anywhere in the United States by calling #211 on your phone, and you will reach a live person during any day or night.

> **NOTE:** *The resources section offers information on organizations and other sources that can support you.*

Churches and Spiritual Centers

If you become economically challenged, it can seem very daunting. However, there are always good people out there supporting those in need. Most towns and cities have churches or spiritual centers. Thanks to hard-working men and women who want to help others, many churches or spiritual centers may offer financial help in different ways. They may provide free meals, have a food/clothing pantry, or send people out to help you.

Churches or spiritual centers may have a collection that is specific to helping those in need. While it may feel awkward to reach out for help, many people have experienced economic hard times. Later, if you feel compelled to give back, you can always do so when you are ready. The bottom line is getting back on your feet and becoming encouraged. You may end up meeting someone who can offer you a job or connect you to a resource you need. I always ask my clients, what is the most loving and empowering thing you can do right now? Answer that question for yourself when you need a little extra self-love and care.

Budgeting and Getting Out of Debt

One of my clients' most significant concerns involves what happens after being fired or when about to be fired from a job. Loss of income can be terrifying or concerning to anyone. Losing income can also lead to the loss of savings and your 401k plan if you have one. That alone can shake most people to their core and make them feel vulnerable—even cause them to feel a loss of confidence in their future.

If you are fired and/or experience a period of unemployment, you may need some expert guidance to help you with a budget or to get out of debt. There are many financial gurus out there, but the one I like the most is Dave Ramsey. He gives practical advice, and he comes across like a down-to-earth person. He shares on his website that 68 percent of Americans don't budget each month and that they also spend 40 percent of their food budget eating out. Dave also shares that, unfortunately, the word budget has gotten a bad rap. It's basically just a plan. When you budget, you're spending with purpose before the month begins.[18]

Dave Ramsey offers a free budget tool on his website, www.EveryDollar.com. It can be empowering to see where you spend your money when you keep a simple record of your budget. If you need help with a budget or getting out of debt, make sure you find a reputable financial mentor and follow their advice.

In many cases, if you have money in savings, you will probably have an easier time leaving a job you hate or recovering from being fired from your job. Understanding your financial portrait can give you peace of mind even when you have a job. We often have more personal power when we can make wise decisions involving our financial means.

How could you earn money and save money if you got fired or left a job where you weren't treated with respect? (Examples: selling items in your home you don't need or reducing your spending.) Consider other marketable skills you may have. Fill out this space or use your own sheet of paper to write your answers.

CHAPTER FIVE

Employment Discrimination in the Workplace

This chapter discusses:

- Forced arbitration (signed agreement) in a company
- The role of the Equal Employment Opportunity Commission (EEOC)
- Discrimination classes: age, disability, equal pay, genetic, harassment and race/color
- Discrimination stories

Your company may request that you sign an arbitration agreement where disputes are settled with an arbitrator who is brought in by the company. Basically, it is a way to settle disputes that don't involve the court. Often employees think that they can't speak up about discrimination in the workplace. I have good news for you. You can file discrimination charges with a federal agency such as the Equal Employment Opportunity Commission (EEOC), even if you have signed an arbitration agreement.

Case law also now makes clear that the EEOC continues to be fully available to employees as an avenue to assert EEO rights and to investigate in the public interest, regardless of whether the parties have entered into an enforceable arbitration agreement.[19] Don't let anyone make you think you are powerless—you have the power to defend yourself and report discrimination in the workplace, regardless of any arbitration agreements you have signed.

Are you being discriminated against in the workplace? Place a check by each statement that describes or is similar to your experience in the workplace.

☐ 1. Do you feel like you are experiencing derogatory remarks about your age?

☐ 2. Do you feel like you are experiencing insulting remarks about having a disability?

☐ 3. Do you feel you are given equal pay for equal work, whether you are a man or a woman?

☐ 4. Do you feel harassed about your genetic information?

☐ 5. Do you feel like you are experiencing offensive remarks because of your national origin or ethnicity?

☐ 6. Do you feel harassed because of your pregnancy, childbirth, or medical condition, relating to childbirth?

☐ 7. Do you feel like you are experiencing offensive remarks about your color or race?

☐ 8. Do you feel harassed due to your religious beliefs or practices?

☐ 9. Do you feel like you are experiencing sexual harassment or unwelcome sexual advances?

☐ 10. Do you feel like you have experienced any reprisal for filing a discrimination allegation?

If you have checked even one of these statements, you may be experiencing discrimination in the workplace.

The Role of the Equal Employment Opportunity Commission (EEOC)

The Equal Employment Opportunity Commission (EEOC.gov) is responsible for enforcing federal laws that make it illegal to discriminate against a job applicant or an employee because of the person's race, color, religion, sex (including pregnancy, gender identity, and sexual orientation), national origin, age (forty or older), disability or genetic information. It is also illegal to discriminate against a person because the person complained about discrimination, filed a charge of discrimination, or participated in an employment discrimination investigation or lawsuit.[20]

Write about who is discriminating against you and how you feel about it. How are you feeling at this time? For example, express the emotions you feel right now. Use this space or use a separate piece of paper.

Discrimination Stories

I have interviewed numerous people who shared their discrimination stories with me. Perhaps their situation is similar to yours. Some of these stories have successful endings, and some of the people decided that the most empowering things they could do for themselves were to move to a new job or become an entrepreneur. It is not weak to leave a lousy job because you are being harassed or discriminated against in your workplace. It may be the kindest and most empowering thing you can do to help yourself.

I am going to briefly describe each discrimination category per the EEOC guidelines so you can understand the different types of discrimination. I highly encourage you to go to the EEOC website and review each type of discrimination type for more specific knowledge.[21] You can learn more about each discrimination category and the requirements needed to support a claim of discrimination or retaliation for filing an EEOC discrimination case. Keep in mind that you can also contact the EEOC and learn where to file a complaint of discrimination in your state, which could result in a quicker outcome for you.

> **NOTE:** *All names have been changed in the workbook to protect their privacy. You may be able to relate to some of these discrimination stories.*

Andrea's Story

Andrea shared with me that she paid thousands of dollars to be a union member. She felt discriminated against because of her disabilities by her peers and supervisors. I had shared the criteria on the EEOC's website about disability discrimination with her. She chose to report her management about being discriminated against for her disabilities to the EEOC.

While she felt she had supporting evidence to present to the union attorney, he decided he did not want to take her case. Bottom line—she was not represented by a union attorney and did not have the money to hire a private employment attorney to address her situation with the EEOC. She was tired, depleted, and abandoned her pursuit to find justice in her matter. She learned that not all labor unions are going to represent you and, in her case,—a waste of her money.

Andrea moved to a new job while doing her best to heal from the mental and physical harm incurred by experiencing perceived workplace discrimination. I will later discuss the importance of documenting "everything" that is relevant when pursuing a workplace discrimination matter.

> **NOTE:** *Learn everything you can about union memberships. There are some great unions that support employees and unfortunately, some not-so-great unions. Attend union meetings and ask to see their financial reports. Pay attention to how union finances are spent. It's up to you to make wise choices if a union is a good idea for you. It's especially important to make sure that union officers are well trained so they can help you in your time of need. Many union will require a year commitment, so make sure they work for you.*

Age Discrimination (Forty Years Old and Older)

If you are forty years old or over and are being treated less favorably because of your age, you may be experiencing what the Equal Employment Opportunity Commission (EEOC) calls age discrimination. The Age Discrimination in Employment Act (ADEA) forbids discrimination against people who are forty years old or older. The EEOC states that some states do have laws that protect younger workers from age discrimination.

The EEOC states that the law forbids discrimination when it comes to hiring, firing, pay, job assignments, promotions, layoff, training, fringe benefits, or terms of employment. It is unlawful to harass someone with offensive remarks about their age, especially when it's frequent and severe to the point that it creates a hostile or offensive work environment that creates an adverse employment decision such as a target being fired or demoted.

The antagonist can be a supervisor, coworker, or even a client or customer. The EEOC states that the ADEA applies to employers with twenty or more employees, including state and local governments. It also applies to employment agencies and labor organizations, as well as to the federal government.[22]

In 2017, there was a press release that Texas Roadhouse would pay $12 million to settle an EEOC age discrimination lawsuit and furnish other relief. The EEOC filed suit seeking relief for a class of applicants who were denied house positions, such as servers, hosts, server assistants and bartenders, because of their age, forty years and older. As a result of the settlement, Texas Roadhouse changed its hiring and recruiting practices.[23]

Over Forty Years Old and Scared to Update Her Resume

I met a sixty-year-old lady, Barbara, who had worked in many jobs and had many skill sets. She was unemployed at the time of telling me her story. She shared how scared she was of listing dates and her experience on her resume. She was sure she would be discriminated against because of her age, even though she had a lot to offer an employer. This lady struggled to decide what to put on her resume because she wanted to get back into the workforce. Later, she found out that there were employers who valued her expertise and maturity.

Older men and women often offer companies and organizations many years of experience and maturity. Some of the perceptions of older workers are that they are slower, less adaptable to change, and uncomfortable working for someone younger. The truth is that many of them are more knowledgeable and experienced than younger employees. They can also be more patient with other employees.

Disability Discrimination

Not everyone with a medical condition is protected by the law, according to the EEOC. To be protected, a person must meet these requirements:

- A person may be disabled if he or she has a physical or mental condition that substantially limits a major life activity (such as walking, talking, seeing, hearing, or learning).
- A person may be disabled if he or she has a history of a disability (such as cancer that is in remission).
- A person may be disabled if he is believed to have a physical or mental impairment that is not transitory (lasting or expected to last six months or less) and minor (even if he does not have such an impairment). Disability discrimination applies to employers with fifteen or more employees, according to the EEOC.[24]

According to a 2012 EEOC press release, Nevada Restaurant Services, a large Las Vegas based gaming company that operates slot machines, taverns, and casinos in Nevada and Montana, would be required to pay $3.5 million to settle a disability discrimination lawsuit. The US Equal Employment Opportunity Commission (EEOC) filed charges against the company. According to the EEOC, since at least 2012, the company violated federal law by maintaining a well-established companywide practice of requiring that employees with disabilities or medical conditions be 100 percent healed before returning to work.

The company's policy did not allow for engagement in an interactive process or provide reasonable accommodations for disabled employees. The company fired and forced disabled employees and employees associated with someone who had a disability to quit their job. Such alleged conduct violates the Americans with Disabilities Act (ADA) and the ADA Amendments Act of 2008 (ADAAA). The company was required to implement effective ADA training for human resources and supervisory personnel and staff.[25]

Note: *According to the EEOC, the law requires an employer to provide reasonable accommodations to employees or a job applicant, unless it would create significant difficulty or high expense for the employer.*

Disabled Female Veteran

In a previous job, I worked with an African American female named Sandra, who had incurred severe disabilities while on active duty in the Army. Sandra shared her experience and wisdom with me. This lady had worked in the government for nearly twenty years and escaped disability discrimination until her last two years of work. She shared that this government agency was either not knowledgeable or did not care about Title I of the Americans with Disabilities Act (ADA) and the Uniformed Services Employment and Reemployment Rights Act (USERRA). These Acts were put in place to protect veterans from employment discrimination.

She stated that she was unfairly overlooked for promotions on many occasions due to her race. Sandra shared with me that she had received outstanding evaluations and past awards for her work. Although proven to be a stellar employee for this organization, her management tried to keep her from seeking her rightful accommodations due to her physical disability. She was entitled to have accommodations that would allow her to work from home. Her management dragged it out and ignored many of her email pleas for help.

As a minority military veteran, she shared that she had been discriminated against on several occasions when applying for managerial positions or promotions while working at the last government agency. Although she was highly qualified for jobs, the other candidates were selected over her. She later found out through a "discovery" that all the other white employees had less experience and education. They were friends of the management where Sandra worked.

Sandra told me, "I coped with being discriminated against in the workplace by first seeking divine guidance from Almighty God and support from family and friends." She remained calm through her all her experiences and in control. She reported all retaliation incidents because she knew it was bound to get worse before it got better if not reported. She sought professional help to receive a settlement from her company. Today, Sandra advocates for those who have fallen victim to racism.

I could not believe my good luck. This lady had been a former Equal Employment Opportunity manager. I asked her to share some advice that could help others who deal with racial or disability discrimination. Here is her guidance: "The first advice I would give anyone who is being bullied or discriminated against is to document everything to include dates, times, location, parties involved, witnesses and details. Stay calm and rational and always remain in control.

Research your company's anti-discrimination policy and see if it addresses some of the problems you are experiencing. Report any incidents of racism to the Equal Employment Opportunity Commission or at an agency that covers discrimination in your state. Racial discrimination matters may become worse if you don't take some action. Seek legal advice from an employment lawyer who specializes in workplace discrimination because in most cases talking to Human Resource (HR) often leads to retaliation. Remember, HR generally protects the company, not you. Read up on employment and discrimination laws in your state or region and find out what federal laws cover your situation."

According to the United Nations Human Rights, over 650 million people around the world live with disabilities. In every region of the world, in every country, persons with disabilities often live on the margins of society, deprived of some of life's fundamental experiences. They have little hope of going to school, getting a job, having their own home, creating a family, and raising their children, socializing, or voting. Persons with disabilities make up the world's largest and most disadvantaged minority.[26]

Equal Pay/Compensation Discrimination

In the same work, men and women should be given equal pay for equal work according to the Equal Pay Act (EPA). The EEOC further states that these jobs do not have to be identical, but they must be substantially equal. It is the job content that determines whether jobs are substantially equal. This includes all forms of pay salary, bonuses, overtime pay, stock options, profit sharing, life insurance, vacation, holiday/leave pay, hotel accommodations, reimbursement for travel expenses, and other work-related benefits.

If there is a violation of this nature, an employee can go directly to the court and is not required to file an EEOC charge beforehand. Employers face responsibilities and accountability when they have fifteen or more employees under Title VII and ADA, twenty or more employees under ADEA, and mostly all employers under EPA.[27]

According to a 2018 EEOC press release, Spec Formliners paid $105,000 to settle the EEOC equal pay lawsuit. A female sales representative received less pay than her male coworker, the federal agency charged.[28]

Paid Less Than the Other Sex

Betty worked in a private company selling bicycles. She was the only female and had the same work duties as the men in this company. One day, she was talking to one of her male coworkers and discovered he was making several dollars more than her. They had started on the same day with no prior skills. She ended up leaving the company and later learned that she might have experienced equal pay discrimination. I suggested she read the EEOC's description of "equal pay." Now she is aware of how to address matters like this one if it ever comes up again.

Genetic (Hereditary) Discrimination

Title II of the Genetic Information Nondiscrimination Act of 2008 (GINA) prohibits genetic information discrimination in employment. This Act includes information about an individual's genetic tests or their family members, along with information about the materialization of a disease or disorder in an individual's family members, also known as family medical history. It is illegal for employers, labor organizations, joint labor-management training staff, and apprentice program staff to make employment decisions or restrict employees' genetic information.[29]

Covered entities are prohibited from disclosing genetic information about applicants, employees, or members. Genetic information must be kept confidential and in a separate medical file. Employers face genetic employment responsibilities and accountability when they have fifteen or employees.[30] According to a 2016 EEOC press release, BNV Home Care Agency paid $125,000 to settle the EEOC genetic discrimination lawsuit; Home Care Provider had unlawfully asked its employees and applicants for genetic information, the federal agency charged.

The company engaged in the unlawful practice of collecting employees' and applicants' genetic information by asking them questions about their family medical history on an employee health assessment form. Such alleged conduct violates the Genetic Information Non-Discrimination Act (GINA), which protects individuals against employment discrimination based on genetic information, including family medical history.[31]

Questionable Genetic Questionnaire

Tom shared with me that he applied for a job in which the company required him to indicate if he or his family had a medical history for certain diseases and disorders. He became suspicious that the company should not be asking him questions of this nature. Tom decided not to answer the job application paperwork and found another job. In hindsight, I shared with Tom that he could have contacted an attorney or the EEOC. An employment attorney or the EEOC can address matters like this to determine if Tom experienced discrimination based on his genetics.

Harassment

According to the EEOC, the employer is automatically liable for harassment by a supervisor that results in a negative employment action such as termination, failure to promote or hire, and loss of wages. If the supervisor's harassment results in a hostile work environment, the employer can avoid liability only if it can prove that: 1) it reasonably tried to prevent and promptly correct the harassing behavior, and 2) the employee unreasonably failed to take advantage of any preventive or corrective opportunities provided by the employer.

According to the EEOC, harassment discrimination violates Title VII of the Civil Rights Act of 1964, the Age Discrimination in Employment Act of 1967, and the Americans with Disabilities Act of 1990. Harassment is defined as unwelcome conduct based on race, color, religion, sex (including pregnancy), national origin, age (forty or older), disability or genetic information. When offensive conduct becomes a condition of continued employment, or the conduct is severe or prevalent enough to create a work environment that a reasonable person continues intimidating, abusive, or hostile, it is unlawful.[32]

The employer is responsible for harassment if they knew or should have known about the harassment and they failed to take timely, appropriate corrective action. Employers face harassment employment responsibilities and accountability when they have fifteen or more employees under Title VII and the ADA or thirty or more employees under the ADEA.[33]

Race/Color Discrimination

When people are discriminated against because of race or personal characteristics associated with their race (skin color, hair texture, or facial features), it is called race/color discrimination. Furthermore, discrimination based on a person's skin color complexion is called color discrimination. It becomes unlawful when there is discrimination involving all aspects of employment, such as hiring, pay, promotions, job assignments, firing, layoff, benefits, and other terms of employment.

Unlawful measures to harass a person's color or race with frequent and severe derogatory remarks, racial slurs, or displaying racially impertinent comments that create adverse employment actions such as demotion or being fired are illegal. Employers are required to be mindful that a no-beard employment policy to all employees without regard to a person's race is unlawful if it is not job-related and necessary to operate the business.

For example, African American men are predisposed to a skin condition that creates severe shaving bumps. Employers face race/color employment responsibilities and accountability when they have fifteen or employees.[34] According to a 2018 EEOC press release, Aqua Resources paid $150,000 to settle an EEOC racial harassment and retaliation suit. The water company fired the foreman because he complained about racial slurs.[35]

African American and Discriminated

How does it feel to be discriminated against because you are African American, but a potential employer thinks you are white? I met an African American female, Mary, who told me that she often gets mistaken for being a white applicant when she gets called for a job interview. Because her last name is one most people likely associate as a "white" name, not an African American or black name, the potential employer wouldn't assume her color either way. Even though she grew up in the South, her accent can hardly be called Southern.

Her skillsets are extremely attractive to employers. She shared with me that many employers had looked shocked when she showed up for a scheduled job interview. While they have never told her that they thought she was white, the expression of shock is hard for these employers to hide when they see this lady in their office for the first time. They were expecting a white job applicant, according to Mary. She stated that she often was not hired when it was a mostly white company.

She also shared with me how hard it is to be African American and economically challenged. Mary grew up in a large city; she felt like she has experienced racial discrimination when she has reached out for different services in her hometown. When I asked her for wisdom on how African Americans can get ahead in the workforce, she stated, "they must work harder to get promoted."

She expressed how tired she is dealing with racial discrimination. Fortunately, she works for a large insurance company that celebrates diversity and even has internal support groups for their employees. For example, if she were experiencing discrimination for being gay, this company has an LGBT support group that would address her matter with management. Her company is a benchmark for other companies to create programs that support diversity in the workplace.

People of Color Discrimination

According to a CNN/Kaiser Family Foundation poll on race in America, 69 percent of blacks and 57 percent of Hispanics say past and present discrimination is a major reason for the problems facing people of their racial or ethnic group. And 26 percent of blacks and 15 percent of Hispanics said they felt that they had been treated unfairly because of their race or ethnicity at their place of work in the past thirty days. But proving discrimination is another thing. In 2014 alone, the EEOC received 31,073 charges alleging race-based discrimination but dismissed 71.4 percent of them due to a lack of reasonable cause.[36]

Male Minority in the Work Culture

David shared with me that he felt like he was discriminated against while he was in the military. He felt discriminated against because of his race. He worked for a female supervisor in Italy who excluded him from different activities because he did not fit in with the white people. Many of them listened to country music and were not open to other types of music. Despite the exclusion, he still outstandingly performed his duties, but when it came to his annual performance evaluation, this female supervisor downgraded his performance rating. When you are vying for promotions as a Senior Noncommissioned Officer, this is like a death sentence or a promotion denial.

This African American male sergeant had always been a stellar worker and recognized for his skill sets. He had won many awards in his career. He was handpicked to work in special duty assignments because of his professionalism. When you are trying to get promoted as an enlisted man or woman, you must have outstanding performance evaluations to move into the top three ranks. It took years for him to get promoted to the advanced enlisted ranks. He had lost the ability to have a fair chance of getting his next promotion in a fair and timely manner.

I have witnessed countless good ol' boy and girl groups that only promoted their favorite people in the military and in the civilian sector of workplaces. It is more common than people realize. Hard work does not always equate to getting a fair outcome in a job. Thankfully, this worthy man did get promoted and stayed positive throughout the whole ordeal. He never lost sight of working towards his next promotion. David received a promotion under a different supervisor who saw him as a valuable employee.

CHAPTER SIX

More Protected Discrimination Classes and Stories

This chapter discusses:

- More discrimination classes: religion, sex-based, pregnancy, national origins, sexual harassment, and retaliation
- More discrimination stories

Religious Discrimination

When a person is treated unfavorably because of their religious beliefs or sincerely held ethical or moral beliefs, this is called religious discrimination. This behavior also includes treating someone differently because of their association or marriage to an individual of a particular religion. Employers are forbidden to discriminate when it comes to any work situation such as hiring, job assignments, promotions, firing, layoff, benefits, or all other conditions of employment.

It is unlawful to harass a person because of their religion. Frequent and severe abusive remarks about a person's practices or beliefs constitute harassment. Title VII also prohibits job or workplace segregation based on religious garb, grooming practices, and religion. It is also unlawful to assign an employee to a non-customer contact position because of feared or actual client or customer preference. Employers must reasonably accommodate an employee's religious practices or beliefs unless it requires more than a minimal burden on the company's business operations.

Employers do not have to accommodate an employee's practices or religious beliefs if it creates a hardship, according to the EEOC. Examples of creating a hardship include if a religious accommodation compromises workplace efficiency, if it poses a safety hazard, infringes on the rights of other employees, or creates more burdensome or hazardous work. Last, employees cannot be forced to participate or not participate in a religious activity as part of their employment. Employers face religious employment responsibilities and accountability when they have fifteen or more employees.[37]

According to a 2018 EEOC press release, J.C. Witherspoon paid $53,000 to settle an EEOC religious discrimination lawsuit. The logging company fired a Hebrew Pentecostal truck driver because of his Sabbath requirement.[38]

Young White Male—Religious and Determined

An older man named Alford told me that when he was a young boy, he worked at a local grocery store in Pennsylvania. As a young man of faith, he chose to wear religious badges on his clothing. One day his manager pulled him aside and told him that he could no longer wear these badges as it offended a customer who shopped at this grocery store.

This young boy was determined to display his faith regardless and went shopping to find something he could wear to support his beliefs. He told me that he heard the voice of God telling him to purchase a pin in the store that he was shopping in at the time. The pin was non-descriptive, but it meant something to this young lad. It was his way to express his faith in a visible and honorable way.

The manager noticed the pin and accepted that this young man was faithful and determined to express his love for God. One day, the man who complained about this young boy's religious badges approached him and asked for the pin's meaning. The boy's comments visibly upset him, and the customer took off in a hurry. The manager told this young man that he could accept the customer being upset.

The young lad had respectfully obliged the customer and gave him his response to the meaning of his pin. Years later, the young boy would run into this customer at a fairground in Pennsylvania. He told me that when he recognized this man that he felt uncomfortable and wanted to head in a different direction. The man approached him and pointed at him and shared with him that he had helped him find God. This behavior from the other man made the young man extremely happy and grateful.

Employees may only value their own religious beliefs or treat those who believe differently from them with disdain. According to EEOC guidelines, the law requires an employer or other covered entity to reasonably accommodate an employee's religious beliefs or practices, unless doing so would cause more than a minimal burden on the operations of the employer's business. This requirement means an employer may be required to make reasonable adjustments to the work environment to allow an employee to practice his or her religion. Examples of some common religious accommodations include flexible scheduling, voluntary shift substitutions or swaps, job reassignments, and modifications to workplace policies or practices. You can learn more about religious discrimination by going to the EEOC website.[39]

Sex-Based Discrimination

When a person is discriminated against as an applicant or employee because of their sex, it is called sex-based discrimination. This discrimination class also includes transgender status, gender identity, or sexual orientation. It is discrimination because of sex violation of Title VII. The law forbids all conditions of adverse employment conditions that discriminate around hiring, pay, promotions, job assignments, firing, layoff, benefits, training, and any other terms of employment. It illegal to harass a person because of their sex. Harassment can include requests for sexual favors, verbal/physical harassment of a sexual nature, or unwelcome sexual advances. The target and antagonist can also be the same sex.

Harassment becomes illegal when there is frequent or severe aggravation that creates an offensive and hostile work environment or when it results in adverse actions such as the target being demoted or fired. It is illegal if employment practices or policies applied to everyone, regardless of sex, have a negative impact on the employment of a certain sex and are not vital to business operation or job-related. Employers face sex-based employment responsibilities and accountability when they have fifteen or more employees.[40]

According to a 2018 EEOC press release, "Dollar General settled an EEOC sexual harassment lawsuit for $70,000 in Red Banks, Miss. The store ignored complaints about the manager's abuse of female employees." According to EEOC's lawsuit, SOCI hired Lori Bowersock in 2006 to perform human resources work. In 2009, Bowersock assumed the human resources manager role for SOCI after her male predecessor's employment ended. At that time, SOCI's executives and management personnel introduced Bowersock to employees and others as the company's human resources manager, EEOC alleged. However, Bowersock performed substantially equal work to that performed by her male predecessor, who was paid more than her, EEOC said. The agency also alleged that SOCI was biased against females and permitted them to be subjected to derogatory sex-based comments in the workplace.[41]

Female Transgender Person and Now an Entrepreneur

How would it feel to be fired after being offered a promotion in a job? I met a transgender woman named Anne, who shared with me that many times the discrimination starts once a person decides to transition from one gender to the other while working their original job. HR fired Anne for lying about her gender, she feels. This woman was in a management position in her job. She was being promoted to a better job when a coworker who also wanted the position did a web search and discovered Anne was transgender.

Anne said the spiteful coworker told everyone at work, which resulted in a meeting with several HR personnel. She told me she was fired due to deceiving them about her gender, even though Anne had an official name change and gender marker on her driver's license that expressed she was a female. Naturally, she felt angry and disappointed because her gender expression had nothing to do with her ability to do the job.

Anne told me that she thinks that her community has a long way to go in educating people about transgender issues. Since this experience, she has given several workshops for HR managers to help educate them on how to understand the proper way to interview a person who is transgender. She has also taught HR personnel how to be an ally and supportive if a person wants to transition while on the job. It can be done with success when HR understands how to support people who are transgender.

In hindsight, she shared with me that she wished she had made a bigger deal out of her negative experience. She further states that she could have reached out to HR personnel, with the hope of educating them and showing them that being transgender is not a big deal. She is happier now as she opened her own business and knows that she will never have to experience that type of discrimination again in the workplace. Today, she is an advocate and mentor for other transgender people.

I asked Anne what advice she would share with other people who are transgender. She stated, "I feel with the recent focus on transgender people in the spotlight the best advice for other transgenders is to be open about your gender with the HR hiring manager. Do not be aggressive but present yourself in a manner where you want to work with them positively to achieve a great outcome.

"As we have all had to teach our doctors about our health needs, we might have to educate the hiring managers, supervisors, and even coworkers about transgender. After we put our human face on transgender, we usually find allies in others. To the HR professional, I want to point out my community is filled with educated and talented individuals who are great employees. Plus, due to the amount of discrimination we have all endured, if you show us respect and treat us like you treat everyone else, you will find yourself with a loyal and hardworking employee who will stay with the company and grow into a great leader."

Sex Discrimination

Although Title VII of the Civil Rights Act of 1964 does not explicitly include sexual orientation or gender identity, the EEOC and courts have said that sex discrimination includes discrimination based on an applicant's or employee's gender identity or sexual orientation. For example, it is illegal for an employer to deny employment opportunities or permit harassment because:

- A woman does not dress or talk in a feminine manner.
- A man dresses in an effeminate manner or enjoys a pastime (like crocheting) that is associated with women.
- A female employee dates women instead of men.
- A male employee plans to marry a man.
- An employee is planning or has made a gender transition from female to male or male to female.[42]

Secretively White Male Gay Manager

I am fortunate to know a genuinely nice man named Ronald, who shared that he is incredibly careful about acknowledging that he is gay to the general public. He shared with me that working in the deep South, where many people are socially conservative, and their religion defines homosexuality as a sin against God. He stated that he never wanted anyone to have leverage over him as an employee or as a manager. He works with conservative men that are known to be tough, such as construction workers. Knowledge of this man being gay could lead to harassment and other problems.

This man does not want anyone to have any leverage so that they can create problems for him. He mentioned that straight people do not walk around in the workplace, announcing that they are straight, so why should gay people walk around and declare that they are gay? Everyone is entitled to their privacy and should be mindful of what they share in the workplace. He further stated that when people found out that he was gay in previous jobs, they would go elsewhere for business. This issue has created a loss of money for him too. Since then, he has determined the best strategy is to keep his sexual preference to himself and a few trusted friends.

Pregnancy Discrimination

Women who are unfavorably discriminated against because they are pregnant or are having a medical condition related to pregnancy or childbirth or because of childbirth constitutes pregnancy discrimination. Discrimination is forbidden based on pregnancy when it comes to all aspects of employment, such as hiring, job assignments, promotions, layoffs, training, benefits, insurance, and firing.

Employers or other covered entities must treat a pregnant woman, who is temporarily unable to perform her job due to pregnancy or childbirth, the same way as they treat other temporarily disabled employees. For example, an employer may have to provide unpaid leave or light duty to accommodate a pregnant woman. If a woman develops gestational diabetes or preeclampsia, which is the pregnancy-induced protein I in the urine and hypertension, it may be considered a disability under the American with Disabilities Act (ADA).

It is unlawful to harass a woman because of her pregnancy, childbirth, or medical conditions relating to these conditions. When harassment is frequent and severe and results in adverse actions such as the target being demoted or fired, it becomes illegal. Foster and adoptive parents may be eligible for twelve weeks of leave, which may be paid or unpaid according to the employee's leave/vacation accrual. Employers face pregnancy employment responsibilities and accountability when they have fifteen or employees.[43]

According to a 2018 EEOC press release, a LA Louisiane restaurant settled an EEOC pregnancy discrimination lawsuit for $82,500. The Los Angeles Cajun restaurant and nightclub denied pregnant servers work according to the federal agency. According to the EEOC's lawsuit, LA Louisiane violated federal law when it reduced the working hours of one of its servers after learning she was pregnant, eventually removing her from the schedule entirely.

The company then refused to allow her to return her to work after giving birth. The EEOC also charged that other servers for LA Louisiane experienced similar discrimination during their pregnancies. Such alleged conduct violates Title VII of the Civil Rights Act of 1964, as amended by the Pregnancy Discrimination Act.[44]

High-Risk Caucasian Pregnancy and Discriminated

Unfortunately, some females face discrimination when they are pregnant. For example, Susan told me that when she was pregnant for the fifth time, it was a high-risk pregnancy. She had already experienced four miscarriages before this pregnancy. Her doctor requested that she work no more than four hours a day due to the possibility of losing this child. This lady provided medical documentation to her managers, who, in turn, gave her an ultimatum of quitting or being fired. The managers of this company, which is a large chain-store, were not empathetic to her medical needs.

At this time, this young female was unaware of her employment rights and quit her job so that she would not experience the humiliation of being fired. At the time, she was incredibly stressed about the possibility of another miscarriage. Her biggest concern was carrying her pregnancy to full term and delivering a healthy baby. She was not aware of the Pregnancy Discrimination Act (PDA).

National Origin Discrimination

When employees are treated unfavorably or mistreated because they are from a particular country or part of the world because of their ethnicity or accent or they appear to be a particular ethnic background, this is called national origin discrimination. This behavior violates The Immigration Reform and Control Act (IRCA) of 1986. This discrimination can also apply to people who are married or associated with a person of a certain national origin.

It is unlawful to be not hired for employment, fired, promoted, laid off, not trained, or any other condition of employment according to the laws of national origin discrimination. Employers can require an employee to speak fluent English if it is necessary to perform the job productively and safely. Employers face national origin employment responsibilities and accountability when they have fifteen or more employees.[45]

According to a 2016 EEOC press release, the EEOC sued Winner Ford for national origin discrimination because the car dealership paid all Chinese technicians less than non-Chinese. The EEOC charged that since the company's hires in 2010 and 2011, all Chinese EAI technicians started at a lower hourly wage than any other non-Chinese employees with the same job and title. While all EAI technicians performed the same role, non-Chinese EAI technicians continued to earn upwards of $3 more per hour than Chinese EAI Technicians, including those hired after 2011 with inferior or no electrical or auto bodywork experience.[46]

Heavy Foreign Accent

Joseph was born in Nicaragua and had a very heavy accent. When he worked at a local mill on an assembly line, his coworkers mocked his accent. Joseph shared with me a typical day of harassment due to his thick accent. The harassment increased to what he described as a hostile work environment. Coworkers and supervisors gave him a hard time and mocked Joseph daily. They talked with sarcasm as they mocked his foreign accent.

One day he came to work and was pulled into his Human Resources department and was accused of being a poor employee, then fired from his job. He had never been written up or admonished for anything in his work. He shared with me that he was trying to support himself and make a better life for his parents back in Nicaragua. However, after a time, he found a new position and is much happier. Joseph shared with me he would never allow another employee or employer to discriminate against him now that he knows it's illegal.

Sexual Harassment

It is illegal to harass an individual who is a job applicant or employee because of that individual's sex. Examples of harassment include unwelcome sexual advances, requests for sexual favors, sexual harassment, and physical or verbal harassment of a sexual nature. The offensive comment about a person's sex can also constitute harassment. The target and antagonist can also be of the same sex. Severe or frequent harassment is illegal when it creates an offensive or hostile work environment or when it results in adverse employment actions such as a victim being demoted or fired. Employers face sexual harassment employment responsibilities and accountability when they have fifteen or more employees.[47]

According to the EEOC, Draper Development LLC was required to pay $80,000 to settle a sexual harassment suit. According to the federal agency, a former general manager at Subway franchise in Rotterdam sent texts to two seventeen-year-old girls offering jobs in exchange for sex. In addition to paying $80,000 to the two victims, the company was required to distribute a revised policy prohibiting sexual harassment, conduct anti-harassment training for managers and employees, post a public notice about the settlement, and report all sexual harassment complaints to the EEOC.[48]

Sexual Harassment in the Job

Bethany shared with me that she worked in a mostly male work environment. Her leadership turned a blind eye to the fact that her male supervisor was putting pressure on her to go out with him. She kept telling her supervisor that she was not interested in him and wanted a professional working relationship.

She was often the best salesperson in her company. However, it seems like the leadership of this company saw a lawsuit building in front of their eyes. Her supervisor fired Bethany and accused her of being a bad employee, even though she had always outperformed others in this company. She deleted every sexual oriented text from him because she did not want them on her phone. In hindsight, she realized she could have shared the texts with an attorney who would discern whether she had a sexual harassment case. She could have also contacted the EEOC for guidance. She shared with me that she learned her lesson—document, document, and document.

Retaliation

According to the EEOC, retaliation is the most alleged discrimination in the federal sector and the most common discrimination finding in federal sector cases. It is prohibitive to punish job applicants or employees for asserting their rights of employment discrimination, to include harassment according to EEO laws. These EEO rights place an employee in a protected activity status. It is unlawful for employees to receive retaliation as a job applicant or employee. Here are some EEOC samples of retaliation:

The EEOC prohibits punishing job applicants or employees for asserting their rights to be free from employment discrimination, including harassment. Asserting these EEO rights is called protected activity, and it can take many forms. For example, it is unlawful to retaliate against applicants or employees for:

- filing or being a witness in an EEO charge, complaint, investigation, or lawsuit
- communicating with a supervisor or manager about employment discrimination, including harassment
- answering questions during an employer investigation of alleged harassment
- refusing to follow orders that would result in discrimination
- resisting sexual advances, or intervening to protect others
- requesting accommodation of a disability or for a religious practice

- asking managers or coworkers about salary information to uncover potentially discriminatory wages.[49]

According to a 2018 EEOC press release, "Plastipak Packaging was required to pay $90,000 to settle an EEOC retaliation suit. The Plastics manufacturing company fired a materials handler because she complained about sexual harassment."[50] The EEOC held Plastipak Packaging responsible for retaliation.

My experience with retaliation as a whistleblower

After I filed a disability discrimination case with the Veteran Affairs, I alleged numerous retaliation charges. For example, I needed a Reasonable Accommodation to be able to work at home because of my disabilities and was denied this request, as I mentioned earlier in the book. I knew other employees were working from their homes and that they had followed all the same protocols of the American Disability Act mandates as I did. I informed my case manager, who addressed my grievance, and he added all my alleged retaliation charges to my original case. I later received a settlement from the Veteran Affairs after reporting numerous incidents of retaliation.

I have covered the "protected" discrimination classes per the EEOC. It's important to understand the different classes of discrimination.

NOTE: *If you have experienced discrimination, you may feel a range of emotions—sadness, anxiety, PTSD, or depression. It may also seem unconscionable that someone would treat you with disrespect. You have the power within you to help yourself.*

What is the most empowering and kind thing that you can do for yourself at this time? Write about it below. Take your time and think about all the things that can energize you and help you feel better. For example: take a nap, exercise, or talk to a good friend.

CHAPTER SEVEN

Documenting Your Workplace Bullying or Discrimination Matter

This chapter discusses:

- The importance of properly documenting work issues (bullying/discrimination)
- How to document an incidence of bullying or discrimination
- How to send a "clarification" email to Human Resources, your manager, or your supervisor
- Samples of emails to Human Resources, your manager, or your supervisor
- How long to wait for responses on your emails to Human Resources, your manager or supervisor

Daniel Ellsberg, who was employed by RAND Corporation, triggered a national political controversy when he released the "Pentagon Papers," which were a top-secret study of US government decisions about the Vietnam war to the *New York Times* and other newspapers. Ellsberg was charged under the Espionage Act of 1917, along with additional charges of theft and conspiracy. He faced a maximum sentence of up to 115 years. All charges were dismissed due to government misconduct and illegal evidence-gathering. In 2018, Ellsberg received the Olaf Palme Prize for his profound humanism and exceptional moral courage.[51]

In a recent article, "Veteran CIA Analyst: What if Ignored COVID-19 Warnings Had Been Leaked to WikiLeaks?" Ellsberg said, "The name of the game is documents."[52] Daniel Ellsberg's most insistent advice to leakers is: "Always bring documents." Ellsberg presents the importance of documentation in his quote. The reason I brought up the incident and quote by Ellsberg is that documentation represents communication that can prove innocence or capture incidences of negative experiences in the workplace.

This chapter is all about how to record when bullying takes place. I was able to hold my bullies accountable because of detailed discrimination documentation that I wrote and later presented to the Equal Employment Opportunity Commission (EEOC). Often, people believe that they must have a witness, to have a good outcome under their circumstances. Witnesses often fear being fired or facing retaliation if they support you. I never presented a witness in my case with the EEOC. I have worked with clients who felt they were discriminated against or bullied, and they had no witnesses. Objective and well-written documentation may help you receive a better outcome. You may not need a witness. I am not joking.

> **NOTE:** *Witnesses are often afraid of retaliation for defending you or sharing the details of what they saw in the workplace. This workbook will offer templates you can use to document your "email" trail.*

I mentioned earlier in this workbook that bullying is not presently illegal. However, you can still document what happens to you and use it in the hope of receiving a fair outcome. I also want to emphasize how important it is to document incidences of incivility and discrimination. Remember Tanya? She was the lady who felt sexually harassed in her workplace. I shared her story earlier in the book.

Tanya experienced numerous incidents of harassment from a man in the company where she worked whom she did not want to date. The offending man would touch her shoulders or her neck, even though Tanya asked him to stop. He became more aggressive with her each day. She would call me and cry on the phone over her dilemma. It was clear to me that the illegal behavior was impacting her in an extremely negative manner.

I shared with her how to document her sexual harassment incidences so that she would have evidence to present an employment attorney if things did not get better. She hoped that the problems would go away. The problems only got worse as the man harassed her so severely that she was having nightmares, trouble sleeping, and escalating health issues. She became deeply depressed. Perhaps the leadership caught on to what was happening in the company. They started writing Tanya up for all kinds of performance issues, which had never been a problem in the past.

She was a great employee and had received many awards and incentives that recognized her contributions to the company. One day, she was called into the HR department and fired. Tanya's managers told her that she was not meeting company performance standards. Perhaps the leadership saw the possibility of litigation, and they chose to take the easiest and most unethical route. They fired Tanya and kept the man that had been sexually harassing Tanya.

Tanya's managers fired her shortly after she brought her complaints to the management. She contacted me and told me that she should have documented the sexual harassment. She shared that she should have followed my guidance on how to document and report the matter. She further stated that she would hire an employment attorney so that they could pursue legal action against the company. I proceeded to ask her what evidence she would present to the employment attorney. I was curious of the evidence or proof she would give to the employment attorney to review and assess if there was proof of sexual harassment.

Unfortunately, Tanya had no evidence or a documentation trail to provide to an attorney. Tanya had no evidence of any kind because she did not document the matter and had hoped that things would get better. She deleted texts from the man that may have proven sexual harassment because she did not want them on her cell phone. When a company manager takes no action to prevent or correct incivility or discrimination in their workplace, it sets a terrible example for everyone.

Tanya moved on to another company and experienced sexual harassment again. This time, she employed the documenting skills I had taught her. The harassment ended. She decided to move to another job anyway because the memories upset her. In her new job, she felt more comfortable and did not experience any more harassment.

NOTE: *Never store documentation on your work computer. Someone may be able to access and read your documentation. Worse—delete your emails or other documentation.*

Checklist for documenting workplace bullying or discrimination.

☐ 1. Ensure you use email to communicate and create an "email trail" when you have concerns about being mistreated in the workplace.

☐ 2. Ensure you write brief and objective emails when you discuss your concerns or ask for clarification on past communication.

☐ 3. Ensure you print and keep a copy of your email in a safe place outside of work.

☐ 4. Ensure that you send "clarifying" emails when necessary to your supervisor, HR, EEOC representatives, lawyer, and other agencies involved in your work matter.

☐ 5. Organize your notes, emails, and all documentation in a binder or folder.

☐ 6. If you are seeking medical/mental health care—ensure your medical records tie-in with your discrimination or bullying incidents.

☐ 7. Do not count on a witness alone if you have one. Document... document... document.

Documentation for Unemployment Compensation

I want to stress that accurate and proper documentation may also support you if you get fired and have to fight to receive your unemployment compensation. It is never a guarantee that you will get unemployment if you get fired. You may face an appeal with the Employment Security Commission (ESC) and have to support your claim to be entitled to unemployment compensation if your former management challenges your right to compensation.

In most cases, the management at your old job will most likely ask their Human Resources to represent the company or organization. With the right documentation, you will likely have a better outcome and you get to present your side of the story. Contact your local unemployment office for further details on unemployment compensation. You can find it by searching online.

Perhaps you are going to file an Equal Employment Opportunity (EEOC) claim for discrimination. You may face retaliation or bullying from your employees or supervisors. The evidence you will need must show discrimination or that you received retaliation for reporting your company or agency. You may or may not want to file with the Equal Employment Opportunity Commission or another agency for help with your situation. The choice is always yours.

Still, you may want to use your documentation as leverage to negotiate better terms in your workplace or a settlement from your employer if you have faced adversity. There is an art and science to creating workplace bullying documentation. People often document what's happening in their work environment, but there is more to documenting than simply keeping notes on your work situation.

Documenting Your Issues

Organizing your documentation trail is quite simple. Here are some of the recommended items you will need:

- Binder approximately one to two inches thick
- Dividers to separate your documentation into categories
- Table of contents (emails, medical records, other documentation)

It never fails, because we are human, that some people will stick all their documentation or evidence in a drawer, in one big pile. That may not be a big deal if it's only five pages of documentation. However, if you are collecting larger amounts of documentation, it needs to be organized and easy to access. Take the time to create a binder and file your documentation in a chronological manner based on the date of each item. If you need to present this information to an attorney, judge, unemployment mediator, or other professional—you want to make a good impression. You also want to come across as a credible and organized person. You want to be taken seriously.

Be sure you are documenting the who, what, where, and why of what is happening in your work environment. Keep it very brief, organized, and factual. I can tell you from experience that judges, attorneys, managers, HR departments, etc. will not take you as seriously if you are wordy and very subjective in your documentation. If you decide to work with an attorney—they will want credible and objective details about your work situation. The worst way to start out working with an employment attorney is to give them documentation that is unorganized or not relevant to your discrimination matter.

Documenting your workplace incidents can "trigger" emotional feelings. If you are feeling emotional or unstable, you must reach out to a mental health expert, professional coach, mentor, clergy member, clinician, or a professional expert to get the support you need. You want to be as emotionally stable as possible, so you can effectively communicate with the people in your life. Also, an attorney may be more willing to work with you on a contingency when you have documentation that supports your claim of discrimination and possible retaliation claim.

When an attorney agrees to work with you on a contingency, they have skin in the game and have an investment in your case. You may find this to be highly beneficial. There are times when you will want to have supportive documentation, so you can try to positively influence your employer on compensating you if you have dealt with bullying, discrimination, or retaliation.

I would never depend on a witness because they may get scared and don't want to lose their job or face retaliation for supporting you. Lawyers may get uncomfortable when they don't know how a witness will perform in a courtroom setting or during a legal deposition. Witnesses can become forgetful, change their story, or retract earlier statements. Credible documentation can give you a better chance to receive fair compensation. Let's start by documenting what is going on in your workplace.

Tips on Documenting

Write down the times, dates, people involved, and a brief, objective summary of your workplace bullying experience(s). I suggest you type it out in an email. If you use your work computer—be sure to print it out and hand carry it home. Never email documentation home because your organization may have their Information Technology (IT) department or someone else monitoring your emails. Also, never leave your documentation or notes in your workplace. You never know who may search your desk or file drawers.

You always want to keep your actions and documentation private so that you have the upper hand. There may be a time when you release your documentation to an employment attorney, the Employment Security Commission, an HR expert, or an EEOC administrative judge. If you have reported your peers or supervisors to an agency like the Equal Employment Opportunity Commission or another agency for investigation of your claims and your experience retaliation, you want to ensure that you have been documenting everything relevant to your situation.

Discrimination is no fun, but the good news is that the Equal Employment Opportunity Commission (EEOC) and other agencies like the EEOC, appear to triage their cases. This action means they give the highest priority to the most severe cases, usually cases where a person has received extreme retaliation for reporting discrimination. The more retaliation you receive for filing charges with the EEOC or similar agency--generally speaking--the sooner you may receive your hearing date. Again, you will want to provide documentation that shows you have received retaliation.

Many people know that workplace discrimination can harm people—emotionally and physically. To leverage a better outcome, consider sending each offending person an email stating that their behavior towards you is harming your mental and physical health if it is indeed harming you. Whether or not they respond, print out the email, and hand-carry it to a safe place for storage. What you are doing is setting up a documentation trail that can, later on, show you reached out to your coworkers or supervisors and stated your concerns about your health and wellbeing.

> **NOTE:** *You can talk to the perpetrator or your supervisor, but remember, you want to have proof to show you conducted a conversation with them. If you speak to a supervisor or a perpetrator, send an email that clarifies the discussion you had with them, so you have an email for documentation.*

Here is an example of an email to send to the person who is discriminating against you.

> *Dear Sally,* (USE THE APPROPRIATE NAME)
>
> *You made an offensive remark about my sexuality this afternoon. You made the following remark(s)* _____
> _____.
> *I request that you immediately stop making offensive and derogatory remarks about me. I have the right to work in an environment that is free of discrimination. Your behavior is affecting my health and wellbeing* (IF THIS APPLIES).
>
> *Thank you,*
>
> *Tom* (USE YOUR NAME)

If you feel that their behavior is affecting your wellbeing, be sure to imply that in your email. Be sure to tailor your email to "fit" your situation. Always keep your email correspondence positive and professional. It could be used against you if you come across as confrontational or unprofessional. It's helpful in your case to have these emails as documentation. You may want to provide these emails to an employment attorney if you work with one. You may even consider sending an email to each supervisor, one at a time, to let the supervisor know that you are suffering mentally or physically from the discrimination in your workplace if this is the case.

Do not let your pride get the best of you. You may get laughed at or mocked for sending these kinds of emails, but in the end, you may be smiling when you get a settlement in your favor or receive a favorable outcome.

> **NOTE:** *There may be times when your supervisor, manager, HR, internal EEO specialist may want to talk to you, instead of responding to your email. Your supervisor or manager may tell you to stop sending emails to people relevant to your situation, but remember, if you don't keep up an email trail, you may not have proper proof or documentation of meetings and communication with others.*

Here is a sample of an email you can send to a supervisor if they are bullying or discriminating against you.

> *Dear Mr. Smith,* (USE THE APPROPRIATE NAME)
>
> *On March 3, 20__, you yelled at me in front of my co-workers and called me stupid and incompetent. I would like to express to you that I have the right to work in a respectful environment. If you felt that I had made a mistake, I ask in the future that I have a representative of my choice with me if you want to point out errors you believe I have made. I also ask that I be afforded the right to privacy with you and my representative.*
>
> *The constant yelling or bullying me is affecting my mental or physical health* (IF SO). *I take great pride in my work. This negative behavior can affect the quality of my work because I am feeling stressed by your continual harassment of me. I am asking that the bullying or discrimination stop immediately.*
>
> *Sincerely,*
>
> *Jane Doe* (USE YOUR NAME)

You may be wondering if you should report an incident of abuse to your HR department. It can be a little intimidating because you wonder what the outcome will be. Email them about the incident first or following up with a "clarifying" email. Follow up with emails within forty-eight hours if you do not get a response back from your supervisor, HR, or other personnel. It's crucial to see a professional caregiver or doctor if you are experiencing mental or physical harm. Be sure to ask them to document the harassment or workplace bullying that is happening to you at your job. Your medical records need to reflect that you are experiencing negative (mental/physical) medical issues because of workplace bullying or discrimination. It is especially important to have the medical records tie into the abuse you are receiving from bullying or discrimination.

For example, you want your medical records to state you have filed a lawsuit or an EEOC case against your workplace so that you can present medical records to your attorney or whoever needs medical records to support you receive a fair outcome in your matter. Be sure that you get copies of these records if you are going to present them as documentation.

> **NOTE:** *It's immensely helpful to have your medical records state you are suffering from being harassed or discriminated against in your job if this is the case. If your medical records do not accurately reflect the harm you are experiencing from your perpetrator or don't tie into your litigation case, be sure to ask the medical staff to amend your medical records. This kind of documentation can be useful for an employment attorney or other professional and may support you receiving a fair outcome or settlement.*

Sample Letter to HR or Your Supervisor about Being Mistreated in the Workplace

Here is how you show that you reached out to your HR department. It's essential to create an email trail. Remember to print out your email and keep it in a safe place. Be sure to tailor your email to "fit" your situation.

> *Dear Mrs. Smith* (HR DEPARTMENT) *or Mr. Taylor* (SUPERVISOR) (USE APPROPRI-
> ATE NAMES)
>
> *I am having a bullying/discrimination problem with Sally/Tom. I have
> addressed the matter with her/him on _____. (DATE) The prob-
> lem has intensified, and I am bringing it to your awareness and asking
> for your support. The following is occurring:* _____
> _____
> _____ (KEEP IT BRIEF AND OBJECTIVE.)
> *I am attaching a copy of the email I sent Sally/Tom for your review
> and action. I would like to meet with you to discuss the matter further.
> Thank you.*
>
> *Respectively,*
>
> *Alvin* (USE YOUR NAME)

For example, if you are discriminated against because you fall in in the pregnancy protected class, you want to write a statement of how someone has discriminated against you. The EEOC's website has great examples of discrimination. Check out the resources section to learn more about discrimination classes.

Clarifying Email
Here is an example of a "clarifying" email to send to HR after you discuss your
situation in the workplace.

> *Dear Mrs. Smith* (HR DEPARTMENT) *or Mr. Taylor* (SUPERVISOR),
>
> *For clarification purposes, I want to ensure I understand you correctly.
> Earlier today, you discussed the option of me moving to a new depart-
> ment, so I do not have to work with or around _____. (NAME OF
> PERSON) I had discussed with you that I was being harassed by Tom/
> Sally and that the following occurred:* _____

_____

_____ . (KEEP IT BRIEF AND OBJECTIVE.)

Would you please clarify this to me by email if these statements are correct. Thank you for allowing me to discuss this matter with you.

Respectively,

Bob (USE YOUR NAME)

Be sure to print out the email every time you send it to your HR or supervisors. Take your copy and put it in a safe location, but never leave it at your workplace. The reason you send an email like this is to get a response and to also document (by email) your request for clarification. Never mind if the person you sent the email to doesn't answer—you can still use the email as documentation to show you reached out to this person for clarification or to discuss your issue. If you discuss the matter in person or by letter—you may not have proof that you reached out to HR or your supervisor—follow-up with an email after all meetings with HR.

If you filed a discrimination case with the EEOC, a state-level agency, or in the civilian court system, you are not supposed to receive retaliation after filing charges. If this is the case, you will need to prove that they retaliated against you with evidence.

Email Documenting Retaliation

Here are examples of retaliation emails.

Dear (HR, SUPERVISOR, MANAGEMENT), (USE APPROPRIATE NAME)

I filed an EEOC case on _____ (DATE), *and since then, I received a bad performance evaluation on* _____ (DATE), *but I have consistently met all my performance standards. I was also recognized with a cash incentive for my exceptional performance at work recently. This performance review appears to be retaliatory, and I request a fair performance evaluation of my work.*

Or...

I filed an EEOC case on _____ (DATE), *and since then, you transferred me to a less desirable position* (STATE THE DETAILS). *This behavior appears to be retaliatory. I request to be assigned back to my former work position.*

Or...

I filed an EEOC case on _____ (DATE), *and since then, I have been punished for filing an EEO complaint and have had my work schedule changed to conflict with my family responsibilities. This behavior appears to be retaliatory. I request reinstatement of my former work schedule.*

Respectively,

Danny (USE YOUR NAME)

Remember, the burden of proof is always on you to prove discrimination or retaliation allegations. You get the picture now. You are creating more email trails of documentation.

> **NOTE:** *Any time you feel that that you should be documenting a communication or situation—send an email. Whether it's a bully, a supervisor, HR, a manager, an EEOC representative—document important information with an email. A printed email captures the "story of what is happening at the time. Be sure to add that you are experiencing harm for your wellbeing—if that is the case.*

Comprehensive documentation will always give you a better chance of a positive outcome. It's not a bad idea to photocopy your documents and keep a second secure file. Depending on the circumstances, you never know how desperate an antagonist may become to find your documentation.

Freedom of Information Act (FOIA) for Government Employees

You may want to seek government records, emails, correspondence, etc. that support your bullying or discrimination claim. You can request to get these documents by asking for a FOIA request. Each government agency has similar requirements in obtaining FOIA requests. You can write a letter to your agency explaining in detail what documents/communication you are seeking. There may be a cost to obtaining your FOIA request, so be sure you are specific about what you want to acquire from your agency.

You may be able to obtain some documents without seeking a FOIA request. You can find the FOIA office to each government agency at www.foia.gov. Ask your management or HR by email on how to get records, written correspondence, emails, and more if you work in the private sector. Employment attorneys also know how to request records and documentation from the private and public sectors.

> **NOTE:** *If you choose any other alternative than email, you may not have a trail of communication. Mail and faxes sometimes get lost, even in the best of circumstances.*

Private Sector Records/Documents

If you ask your company for records or documentation that may support your claims of mistreatment, please do it by email. If your company does not co-operate with you, you may have to work with an attorney to seek records or documentation from your company. Often, lawyers may ask for documentation during the "discovery phase" of the EEO process from the employer or their attorney.[53] If this is the case for you—you may have a better opportunity of receiving the documentation you need.

Internal EEO Counselors and EEOC

If you seek help for being discriminated against within your company or agency, you may be working with an internal or agency EEO counselor. Internal EEO staff usually work for the agency director. It's also vital that you keep up the "email trail" if you work with them. If you file discrimination charges at the state level or with the EEOC, stick with the "email trail." That way, you have captured all communication. There will be required forms to fill out, deadlines, and other correspondence. It's easiest and best to request everything be accomplished by email.

> **NOTE:** *There has been a lot of emphasis on keeping an "email trail." You may now understand why it's important to have proof, evidence, and documentation to support your claims of mistreatment. Review all documentation, reports, investigation reports thoroughly to make sure it's accurate. If you find discrepancies—send an email stating the errors in the document.*

Some of my clients that I taught how to "document" their bullying or discrimination matters contacted me to let me know that some of their investigations on their discrimination claims were missing comments that they provided. They were also missing allegations on their discrimination investigations. I remembered one of my clients who signed an investigation report, which was missing lots of "substantial evidence."

Unfortunately, it backfired on her because she signed the report without reading it to ensure accuracy. Her attorney tried to get the allegations through the EEOC system, but my client had signed the investigation report as accurate.

The Administrative Judge (EEOC) reminded her lawyer that she had signed the report as accurate.

It's easy to be frazzled and exhausted if you are dealing with being mistreated in the workplace. The longer the harassment goes on, the likelihood is that stress will affect your health and wellbeing. Long-term stress can lead to chronic health issues. It can impact your friends and loved ones.

> **NOTE:** *Chronic stress from being mistreated in the workplace can wear you out and make you sick. It's vital to keep yourself in the best shape as possible. Workplace bullying and discrimination investigations can last for months and sometimes years.*

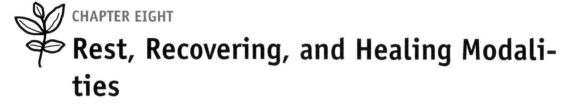

CHAPTER EIGHT

Rest, Recovering, and Healing Modalities

This chapter discusses the following:
- The importance of self-care
- Overcoming mistreatment
- Modalities for your health and wellbeing

The Importance of Self-Care

When people in the workplace mistreat others, it affects each person in different ways. Some people have good coping strategies, while others have none. Everyone handles stress differently. Every client that I have supported has needed to seek professional mental health care. This comment is not to say that you will need it. It's not a matter of being strong or weak—the harm of bullying can take years for you to overcome. Even if you get a positive outcome like a settlement or the option to move to a different job, you may still carry the "mental scars" from the abuse you have suffered from your bullies.

Wouldn't it be nice if you could wave a magic wand and make all the pain disappear? You are probably more capable than you know. With the right tools, you can support yourself in healing and recovery. Earlier in this book, I mentioned that I did not take good care of myself as I was standing up to my bullying and discrimination. Let me explain. When I saw other people speaking out against illegal activities, I witnessed them experiencing extreme harassment.

I even observed good employees quitting their jobs because they were scared. I am a people-person, and I don't like to see anyone mistreated. So, when I received horrific retaliation for reporting my managers, I researched all the laws, policies, and handbooks so I could represent myself with the Equal Employment Opportunity Commission (EEOC). I spent many hours researching and compiling data for my disability discrimination and retaliation case. I had the "mindset" of still being in the Air Force—kept pushing myself until the project was done. The problem was it took nearly two years of documenting and lots of paperwork. My efforts consumed my time and ruined my health.

Don't Be Your Own Worst Bully

Long hours and hard work did pay off, but not without taking an emotional and physical toll on my body. I was obsessed with holding my antagonists accountable; I did not practice self-care during these turbulent times. If I were to go back and change things—I would have exercised more, practiced meditation, gotten more massages, and placed more relaxation modalities into my life. I was hell-bent on standing up for myself and the other employees in my previous job, but there has to be some balance in our lives, or we pay a high price.

When I was in the mental health ward recovering from all the trauma I experienced from my management, I was able to shower on the third day. I had been on anti-depressants and anti-anxiety medicine for some time, and I felt like a zombie. At the time, I realized I was mistreating myself into thinking I was helpless and a victim. I remember feeling even more depressed and hating myself for falling into this trap, but this experience was part of my growth and transformation. I call my experience an epiphany, and I needed it to grow to become more resilient in my life. Adversity can make you more empowered if you find balance in your life, even when there is chaos.

Sleep, Exercise, and Eating Healthy Foods

Many people experience chronic stress from workplace harassment. Lots of people have a hard time sleeping when they have anxiety, or they are fearful of their work issues. It's essential to discuss this with your medical doctor or a qualified expert if you are having sleep problems. There are many natural remedies that can help you sleep better.

It's essential to recognize you need help and may need to follow the medical guidance given to you by your doctor or other medical expert. Dr. Susheel Patil of the Johns Hopkins Sleep Center shares some recommendations for better sleep:[54]

- Consider exercising three to four hours before bedtime.
- Have a wind-down routine of thirty to sixty minutes before you go to bed.
- Go to bed at a regular time each night.
- Wake up at a regular time every morning.
- Avoid naps during the day.
- Avoid alcohol close to bedtime.
- Avoid caffeine after 12 p.m.

One of the easiest ways to relieve stress is to go for a walk or find an activity that you enjoy. Exercise is the way to good health and maintaining good health. Even if you don't feel like walking or doing some other kinds of exercise— please do it for your own wellbeing.

Be mindful of the food you eat—is it healthy or is it adding more problems to your health? You can always reach out to a coach or health expert to find out more about the benefits of living a healthy life.

Conquering Your Story

Have you ever been upset by someone's comments about you? I remember discussing some information with a lady named Betty, who hatefully told me that she did not want to hear my remarks even after asking what was going on in my life. Her comments were very cold and upset me. Her behavior and sarcasm were like a barbed-wire fence slicing into me—very cutting!

I felt warm tears going down my face as I tried to get control of my feelings and tell her that her mean comments hurt my feelings. Eventually, I was able to tell her how I felt about her criticism of what I had said to her. I believe that she felt some remorse for hurting me at the time because I knew she had personal issues that were affecting her too.

After dissecting our conversation, a day later, I felt she had given me what I call a gift in ugly wrapping paper. Her comments triggered memories. I remembered being a seven-year-old child. My Granny Lee had a sharp tongue and often gave me what I called tough love comments as a child. I knew she loved me, but she had grown up in an orphanage and had a little bit of armor on at times. Granny Lee always dressed in a polished manner with her single strand of milky white pearls, and she usually wore a conservative outfit. She had earned her advanced degrees in her later years. My granny always compared IQs of my family members. She seemed to be infatuated with how well we did on the tests she gave each of us. It felt belittling to me.

I was a child who kept the comments of my granny in my subconscious for many years. I did not know any better; I was too young to discern the meanings of my granny's behavior. Today, I am amused when I think of her comments. I genuinely believed it was a "mental" strategy to motivate me to achieve in education.

So, when people made sharp comments to me, I found it very hurtful. I knew I had to heal that little girl in me that sought approval and wanted to be liked by everyone. While it's great to be liked by other people, it's a fact that not everyone will understand or even like you. There are some people in your life that you won't want to spend even five minutes with if you could avoid them.

Receiving Help

I sought hypnotherapy through Sarah Gewanter, who was a psychotherapist and a master hypnotherapist. Sarah hypnotized me and helped me to go back to heal many of my negative childhood experiences. I was able to regress to being a child and ready to discuss my concerns with those who had harmed me. While hypnotized, I was able to tell one of the antagonists that he was wrong for molesting me as a child. My hypnosis sessions were powerful and healing. I will share some healing strategies that have worked for me. Be patient and kind to yourself as you explore strategies that can help you.

Whether you decide to stand up to your workplace bullying situation or choose to leave your job to save your health, this is a time to be gentle with yourself. I will share some holistic modalities that can support your self-care and help you feel your best. There are many other modalities that you may want to explore too.

Hypnotherapy for Changing Your Habits

Hypnosis is like a guided meditation, according to an article on WebMD.com[55] It has many comprehensive benefits that help you gain clarity, confidence, a sense of safety, overcome phobias, fears, anxiety, depression, stress, PTSD, and grief. How does hypnosis work? A hypnotist or hypnotherapist helps the client get into a restful state of relaxation known as a trance. The fundamental difference is that a hypnotist is a non-clinical practitioner, and a hypnotherapist is a clinical practitioner.

You will work with helpful suggestions during your hypnosis session. These could be suggestions to your subconscious that you are feeling better, can handle the stress in your life, or stand up to your antagonist. There are so many powerful suggestions to help you in your time of need. You can come up with suggestions that pertain to your goals or the outcome you wish.

Hypnotherapy can be an aid to psychotherapy or other counseling. It enables the client to work on issues to improve their self-worth and self-confidence. It's also one of the most effective stress-reliever modalities available. Many people report they felt like they woke up from a great nap when they come out of a hypnotic trance. I love it so much that I became certified in 2012 to help others receive the benefits of hypnosis.

My client June told me she was able to write her boss and tell him his behavior was that of an antagonist and that she had moved on in her life. She told me it was very liberating after experiencing so much grief from being bullied. I was so glad that I had taken the time and money to get certified in hypnosis.

Massage

According to the Mayo Clinic, studies of the benefits of massage demonstrate that it is an effective treatment for reducing stress, pain and muscle tension, anxiety, and digestion disorders. If you are dealing with workplace bullying, you probably feel tense, and the stress you are going through can manifest many types of health ailments. Many massage therapists know how to get to the root of the problem when it comes to tight muscles or, you need some stress relief through massage. Massage can assist in easing medication dependence, lessen depression and anxiety, release endorphins—amino acids that work as the body's natural painkiller, and relieve migraine pain.[56]

Massage can be a powerful ally in your healthcare regimen. An estimated 75 to 90 percent of all visits to primary care physicians are for stress-related problems.[57] So, why not consider massage so you can decrease your anxiety, enhance your sleep quality, have more considerable energy, improve your concentration, and reduce your fatigue.

Hiring the Right Life Coach or Mentor

You may be dealing with a work issue at this time or you want to experience a transformation in your personal growth. If so, you may want to hire a life coach or mentor to help you break through some barriers in your life or help you gain clarity on an issue. There are many coaches out there—some with lots of training and some who have taken a weekend course. Some have had no coach training at all. Coaching has many potential benefits if you find the right life coach. Here are just a few:

- Achievement of your personal and professional goals.
- Breaking through blocks or perceived limitations.
- Organization, focus, and achievement of goals.
- Improved personal empowerment and personal power.

- Increased self-awareness.
- Healthier boundaries with others in your life.
- More confidence and self-esteem.
- Higher energy and wellbeing.
- Realization of your gifts and talents and how to use them.

How do you differentiate between all the coaches out there and find the right one for you? Life coaching is a transformative process, where your results are driven by your efforts, relating to your personal goals. Working with a life coach may require regularly scheduled phone or in-person meetings while providing your own self-awareness and accountability.

1 Be sure you know what you want to achieve in hiring a life coach. For example, you may want to overcome fears of moving forward in your life after dealing with traumatic experiences. Many coaches have niches, which helps to define their best type of client, with the work they do as a coach. As a life coach, I like to work with clients who want to find their voices, strengths, and personal power. Many of my clients have dealt with some type of abuse or bullying. They wish to break-through their feelings of being a target or feeling small in their lives.

2 Be sure to research the coach you are thinking of hiring. Ask them for references, and follow up by contacting the references. Trust your gut feelings when researching life coaches. An accredited life coach is often best because they have done the training and are certified in coaching. Life Coaches should never manipulate or bully someone into working with them. Again—trust your gut and think twice about working with them if you feel pushed to work with someone.

3 A life coach is supposed to help you with your transformation or achieving your goals. It's always about your agenda or goals. Be clear about the goals you want to achieve and your availability to work with a life coach.

4 A life coach may ask you to sign a contract to work with them. This request is a professional contract between you and the life coach. They may also want to sell you a month or three-month package too. Don't be afraid to ask if you can pay for one session to see if this life coach is a good fit. In some cases, it will take more than one session to help you to achieve your goal(s). You want to be mindful of your investment in yourself and find the right life coach for your needs.

5 Keep in mind when hiring a life coach, that if it does not work out, you should ask to stop the services between you and the life coach. An ethical

life coach will want what is best for you and most likely will allow you to break the contract. The bottom line is that you want positive results when working with a life coach. Take your time and remember, you are investing in your personal growth and power.

Prozac or a Life Coach/Mentor/Mental Health Professional?

I have mentioned that often bullies will target people who appear weak and easy to harass. The exception is that some people may bully you for reporting them for doing illegal activities or unethical behavior, whether you are a confident person or an insecure person. They may feel threatened and lash out to intimidate you or to push you to leave your job. Help yourself by working on your self-growth and claim your inner strength and personal power. When you demonstrate your strength, there is a good chance of being treated better by others.

If you had the choice, would you choose to take Prozac for mild depression, or would you hire a life coach? According to the World Health Organization (WHO), 350 million people worldwide suffer from depression.[58] It is a leading cause of disability. When it comes to what creates depression, you may want to consider the benefits of Prozac or any other pharmaceutical versus what paybacks you will get from working with a life coach, a mentor, or mental health professional.

It's essential to listen to your doctor and follow their medical advice. If you are dealing with depression, you may need prescribed medicine to manage your depression. It may help you to find stability in your life or to find a way to cope with your depression. But what if you could figure out how to solve some of your problems with the help of a coach or mentor? Sometimes you need another person to show you how you have become your own worst bully.

For example, if you allow others to mistreat or disrespect you, this could cause you to be depressed. Working with a life coach who is well-suited to support your needs and goals can help you to break some habits that aren't contributing to your highest good. If others have bullied you, your self-esteem and self-love may be at an all-time low. No one wants to experience mistreatment; it's plain awful. The mental and physical harm can put you in a state of mind that is hard to overcome. Every person feels their story is compelling. Their perception is real to them.

You can learn how to stand up to workplace bullying and discrimination. Sometimes you have to decide whether to stand up for yourself or to make a decision that makes you feel safe. Don't get me wrong, there is no shame in taking care of yourself and being on medication if you need it. I know how prescription medicine has benefited me on numerous occasions. Please make sound decisions when dealing with your health and wellbeing. Listen to your doctor and heed their advice. In the past, I was on many anti-depressants and anti-anxiety medicine to cope with my hardships. It took some time to realize my own personal growth and wean myself off medicine I no longer needed.

Meditation for Better Wellbeing

The word meditation is derived from two Latin words: meditari (to think, to dwell upon, and to exercise the mind) and mederi (to heal). Its Sanskrit derivation 'Medha' means wisdom. The Merriam-Webster dictionary defines meditation as engaging in mental exercise (concentrating on breathing or repeating a mantra) to reach a heightened level of spiritual awareness.[59]

Zen meditation, aka Zazen, involves focusing on your breath going in and out of your nose. Shikantaza (just sitting) — in this form the practitioner does not use any specific object of meditation; instead, practitioners remain as much as possible in the present moment, aware of and observing what passes through their minds and around them, without dwelling on anything in particular.[60]

The benefits of meditation are stress reduction and better concentration. Plus meditation encourages a healthy lifestyle, helps increase self-awareness, can increase your happiness, increase self-acceptance, and be a benefit to your cardiovascular and immune health. There are different kinds of meditation, and you may find that one type is better than another for you.

Aromatherapy

One of my favorite modalities for stress management is aromatherapy, which involves essential oils made from flower, herb, and tree parts, like bark, roots, peels, and petals. The cells that give a plant its fragrant smell are its "essence." When an essence is extracted from a plant, it becomes an essential oil.[61] Essential oils are compounds extracted from plants. Essential oils are obtained through distillation (via steam and water) or mechanical methods, such as cold pressing.[62]

Aromatherapy can be used topically, by inhalation, and in the bath. Some essential oils need to be diluted with a carrier oil, such as coconut, sweet almond, or olive oil, because they are so potent. One of my favorite carrier oils is jojoba oil. Here are some of my favorite essential oils to manage stress and my well-being: lavender, jasmine, holy basil, sweet basil, bergamot, chamomile, rose, vetiver, ylang-ylang, frankincense, geranium, clary sage, lemon balm, and fennel. I use my essential oils nearly every day and often put them in my diffusers throughout my home. It's always wise to get advice on using essential oils, so you use them safely. Find a reputable resource or a credible book that administers guidance on using the oils. One of my favorite books on essential oil is *The Heart of Aromatherapy* by Andrea Butje. Some essential oils scents are, unfortunately, a trigger for allergies of various kinds, which can turn serious. Please seek guidance with a qualified aromatherapist or medical expert.

Art Therapy for Creativity and Happiness

Art therapy is an established mental health therapy that uses the creative process of art to enhance the artist's mental, physical, and emotional wellbeing. Art therapy can be helpful to encourage people to be creative and in the development of self-awareness plus stress reduction and increase of self-esteem. Treatment with art therapy can help with people deal with depression, anxiety, mood disorders, abuse, and other behavioral problems.

While people have been using the arts to express, communicate, and heal for thousands of years, art therapy only began to formalize during the middle of the twentieth century. Doctors noted that individuals suffering from mental illness often expressed themselves in drawings and other artworks, which led many to explore the use of art as a healing strategy. Since then, art has become an essential part of the therapeutic field and is used in some assessment and treatment techniques.[63]

Energy Work/Reiki

Reiki is the Japanese tradition of energy healing, and it dates back to the early twentieth century. Chakras, the seven energy transmission centers of the body, are described in ancient Hindu texts. Meridians, the energy superhighways of the body, are the road maps on which traditional Chinese medicine practitioners based acupuncture. Although various ancient cultures used different modalities to stimulate the body's natural ability to heal, they all saw internal energy as a powerful force of good.[64] Many people I know love Reiki sessions, They tell me they feel so good and refreshed after their session. Seek an experienced expert and ask for references.

Binaural Beats

Binaural beats therapy requires a person to listen to different sound frequencies for a set amount of time, without any distractions, and in a comfortable space. Research has shown that when a person listens to binaural beats for a recommended time, their brain changes. Researchers believe these changes occur because the binaural beats activate specific systems within the brain. An electroencephalogram (EEG) that recorded people's electrical brain activity listening to binaural beats showed that the effect on a person's body varied according to the frequency pattern used.[65] I find that listening to binaural beats is one of the easiest ways to relax when I want to chill out. Listening to binaural beats is best accomplished by wearing a headphone or earplugs.

Horticultural Therapy

Agricultural and gardening activities are integrated as complementary therapeutic modalities in many private and public psychiatric clinics in the US. An article published in the journal *Psychiatry Investigation* in 2012 reports that wandering in a natural landscape helps with the recovery of psychiatric patients, reduces pain and medication, improves attention and sleep quality, and alleviates agitation, particularly in elderly dementia patients. Groups of depressed adults also showed substantial improvements in horticultural therapy.[66]

I wrote an article for *Western North Carolina Home and Garden* magazine, where I shared my horticultural therapy wisdom. Here are my three condensed tips for standing up to workplace bullying and discrimination with horticultural therapy:

1 Taking care of yourself is vital and absolutely essential. It's quite easy to get anxious or depressed over being treated with disrespect in the workplace. When you are in a garden, it's easy to embrace the sunshine and the diversity of plants that bring you joy.

2 It's effortless to get caught up in the worries of tomorrow. If you love plants, why not become a Master Gardener, or earn a degree in horticulture. Earning my degree in horticulture after retiring from the Air Force, brought me great joy and is a fabulous modality to alleviate stress in your life.

3 Exercise is essential for your health and wellbeing. When you feel stressed, head out to your garden and pull some weeds. The stretching and pulling will help to take your mind off of your troubles, and you receive the benefit of exercising. Walking through nature, especially by water, is very relaxing

for many people. Forest or nature therapy has been proven to decrease blood pressure, inflammation, and give a greater sense of wellbeing.

Forest Bathing or Nature Therapy

Kathleen Forrest, who is a certified as a Forest therapist, with the Association of Nature and Forest Therapy (ANFT) shares, "forest and nature therapy began in Japan in the 1980s. They called it Shinrin-Yoku or Forest Bathing. Forest therapy is a gentle practice that involves moving very slowly and mindfully through nature while soaking it in with all our senses. It is a relaxing experience that connects us to our natural environment through sensory-based invitations. This therapy is not a hike or a plant/tree identification walk. Nature does the healing and the guide opens the door.

Ever since the Japanese began their research other organizations and colleges have been conducting research on the benefits of not only spending time in nature but being guided by a certified leader. A few of the benefits they found include decreased risk of heart attack, mood-boosting effects, as well as decreased inflammation and thus pain. Some guides have been taking groups of veterans on guided walks, and the veterans report the benefits to their quality of life. A guided walk takes approximately three to four hours depending upon the size of the group.

Herbal Remedies and Supplements for Stress

Herbal remedies have been around for thousands of years. Before consuming any herbs, individuals should consult with a doctor, naturopathic doctor, or professional medical staff. The reason is that some herbs may conflict or have a contraindication with a particular prescription medicine you may be taking. An herbalist professional who is qualified to prescribe the right herb for you may recommend chamomile, for example. According to herbalists, it helps to calm frayed nerves and is an extremely mild sedative.

Chamomile has been widely used in children and adults for thousands of years for a variety of health conditions. Today, people use chamomile as a folk or traditional remedy for sleeplessness, anxiety, and gastrointestinal issues such as the upset stomach, gas, and diarrhea. Take caution if you are allergic to ragweed, chrysanthemums, marigolds, or daisies.[67]

While most herbs are very safe, a medical expert's advice is the best way to take care of your health. You may even want to grow herbs to incorporate them in teas, supplements, tinctures, etc. Always consult with a medical professional or credible medical herbalist on taking herbals as alternative care.

Magnesium is a remarkable and safe muscle relaxant and is especially helpful before going to bed, says Carolyn Dean, MD, author of *The Magnesium Miracle* (Ballantine, 2007). Studies show that passionflower reduces anxiety and promotes better sleep and without sedation or grogginess. While Omega-3s may relieve depression and bipolar disorder, omega-3s can also lessen anxious feelings. A study at the Ohio State University College of Medicine, Columbus, found that omega-3s reduced anxiety in sixty-eight people who took supplements for three months.[68]

While holistic care can be highly beneficial, there are times that an employee may need to seek the care of a medical doctor or professional medical staff for treatment. They may need to seek mental health care, also. Find a doctor that is empathetic to your wellbeing and listens to your concerns.

Mindfulness

Mindfulness is the act of being intensely aware of what you're sensing and feeling at every moment, without interpretation or judgment.[69] It is super easy to spend lots of time problem-solving, thinking negatively, or letting your mind race with concerns of the past or future. The Mayo Clinic states that mindfulness exercises can reduce stress, anxiety, depression, negative thinking, and distractions, which can improve your mood.

It can be as easy as slowing down and noticing a flower and the details of the plant. You can sit in a comfortable chair and close your eyes while paying attention to your breathing. The idea is to stay in the moment and not think of the past or the future. Listening carefully to what someone is saying without judgment can be a great exercise. You can find a mindfulness coach who can be instrumental in supporting you to live a more mindful life. Look for an experienced expert and be willing to ask for references.

Praying or Being Still

Each of us may have a different religious, spiritual background or belief system. Often, we only pray when things are bad for us, when it may be beneficial to be grateful for the good things we have in our life. I suggest that you pray or set the intention to become the person you need to become so you can handle all of the things that come forward in your life. I never pray for the problems to go away. I ask for support to become the person who can figure out how to manage an issue that is going on in my life. Each of us are powerful spiritual beings.

At times, I have woken up out of deep sleep to notice angels in my bedroom. You can imagine these figures first scared me, but I got used to them after a while. I believe they show themselves to me to let me know I am loved, protected, and supported to fulfill my soul's journey on this earth. I was delighted to see that angels came in different colors and that I had the honor to witness them. Every one of us can connect with our Creator. I know each of you may have different experiences and trust that you are supported. You may experience your own unique support system from the divine.

Sexual Abuse and Trauma

If you have experienced sexual abuse and have not been able to heal from it, you may likely feel insecure and have low self-esteem or self-love. You may not mix well with others or, you tend to be quieter than others. Unfortunately, some predators prey on vulnerable men, women, and children. The effect of further abuse on someone already harmed can take years to overcome and often requires professional support from a trauma expert or mental health professional.

I experienced sexual abuse as a child. I know it's tough, and it can make you feel very insecure. It took years of recovery and support to overcome my experience. Recovering from the trauma of sexual abuse can take time, but it's well worth the effort to feel whole and healed. You may need to work with a mental health professional or an expert in traumatic healing.

Loving and Respecting Your Self

What if you could learn to love and respect yourself? The chances are you would have healthier boundaries with others. You may learn how to be an observer instead of an absorber (one who absorbs drama) when dealing with antagonists. Learning how to be a non-player in other people's drama is very empowering and liberating. Sometimes the most excellent teachers are the antagonists.

If you don't learn how to set healthy boundaries in your life and genuinely love yourself, you will probably be dealing with unfavorable circumstances over and over in your life. Set yourself free from your old stories and claim peace and happiness.

NOTE: *Keep in mind that you may want to hire an attorney, seek a mental health professional's services, or find an expert to support you. Take your time, get references if needed, and trust your gut when picking people to help you.*

Write about how you could set boundaries with other people or how you could let others know what you need in your life. What restrictions would you set? You can use this sheet or a separate piece of paper. Example: Saying "no" to things you don't want to do for others.

.

When you learn to become empowered, it's like being taught how to fish. Instead of someone giving you fish to eat, you learn to catch your own fish. You become independent and trust yourself. You get the point. Claiming your personal power means holding yourself accountable to make wiser decisions and to get the help you deserve. Many of the famous spiritual leaders in our world have gone through massive transformations to become who they are today. They have experienced abuse, they have overcome, and today, they teach others how to overcome.

CHAPTER NINE

Programs That Can Support You During a Workplace Issue

This Chapter discusses:

- The Family Medical Leave Act (FMLA)
- Documents needed for FMLA.
- Worker's compensation
- Employee Assistant Program (EAP)

Family Medical Leave Act (FMLA)

I have told my clients to look into using the Family Medical Leave Act (FMLA) if they were eligible for it and needed rest, recovery, and healing. It has been the saving grace to help employees take time off and rest while allowing themselves a break from abusive behavior in their workplaces. One of my clients, Allen, used the FMLA to help him take time off to seek numerous medical appointments.

He was suffering from insomnia, ulcers, and anxiety. Allen was able to use all twelve weeks of FMLA, which gave him a break from his hostile work environment. When he came back to his job, he only had two months before he'd retire. Allen told me that he could have never made it to his retirement if he had not used FMLA for rest and recuperation. He had experienced severe harassment from his management while trying to seek medical care. His managers thought he was out of work too much, even though his time off was for medical appointments.

Stressful Work Environment

Stress from workplace bullying and discrimination can harm your health. You may qualify to invoke the Family and Medical Leave Act (FMLA). If your health is declining due to a hostile work environment or workplace bullying, you may want to consider taking time off to get medical care or prescribed rest from your doctor. The Family and Medical Leave Act requires employers with fifty or more workers to provide up to twelve weeks of unpaid leave for an employee coping with a severe illness or caring for a family member who has one, according to the Department of Labor.[70]

You can inquire with your HR department or with a designated official on this matter. Always inquire by email for documentation purposes. I suggest you ask for guidance on this program, but you can also review the FMLA program for yourself, so you understand how the program works. You can learn more about FMLA in the Resources chapter.

As an HR consultant, I have witnessed managers who wanted to prevent their employees from knowing about FMLA because they were afraid of their staff abusing this program, or they were short on staff. The Family and Medical Leave Act (FMLA) is a federal act, signed by President Bill Clinton on February 5, 1993, requiring covered employers to provide employees job-protected, unpaid leave for qualified medical and family reasons. The Wage and Hour Division of the United States Department of Labor administers FMLA. The bill was a major part of Clinton's first-term agenda.[71]

Your employer cannot decide if you are allowed to invoke this program or not. If you qualify and turn in all the required forms and documents required by your HR department, you are eligible to use the program if you meet the criteria of FMLA.

Overview

The FMLA entitles eligible employees of covered employers to take unpaid, job-protected leave for specified family and medical reasons, continuing group health insurance coverage under the same terms and conditions as if the employee had not taken leave. Eligible employees are entitled to twelve work-weeks of leave in a twelve-month period for:

- The birth of a child and to care for the newborn child within one year of birth.
- The placement with the employee of a child for adoption or foster care and to care for the newly placed child within one year of placement.
- To care for the employee's spouse, child, or parent who has a serious health condition.
- A serious health condition that makes the employee unable to perform the essential functions of his or her job.
- Any qualifying emergency arising out of the fact that the employee's spouse, son, daughter or parent is a covered military member on covered active duty.

- Twenty-six workweeks of leave during a single twelve-month period to care for covered service member with a serious injury or illness if the eligible employee is the service member's spouse, son, daughter, parent, or next of kin (military care giver leave).
- Eligible employees in legal same-sex marriages will be able to take FMLA leave to care for their spouse or family member, regardless of where they live. This program ensures that the FMLA will give spouses in same-sex marriages the same ability as all spouses.[72]

Documentation and Records Needed for FMLA

Some employers and coworkers are nosey and want to know about your health and medical concerns. If this concerns you, please understand you don't have to disclose all your medical information to invoke FMLA. According to the Department of Labor, you do not have to turn over your medical records to your employer. Still, the employer has a statutory right to request that an employee provide medical certification containing sufficient medical facts to establish that a serious health condition exists.[73]

Your employer can ask for complete and sufficient medical certification to invoke FMLA-protected leave due to a serious health condition. Make sure you have all the required medical certification; otherwise, your supervisor may require it in writing. Ask your HR department for a checklist of the required documents needed to invoke FMLA. Your employer or HR professional can also contact your health care provider for authentication or clarification of the medical certificate. FMLA guidelines make clear that in no case may the employee's direct supervisor contact the employee's health care provider.[74]

The Department of Labor states that an employer or HR expert cannot request you sign a release or waiver as part of the medical certification process. This situation happened to one of my clients named Valerie when she sought to invoke FMLA in her previous job. Valerie was asked by a staff member to sign a release for all her medical records. Seriously, would you want someone reading years of your medical records? There is guidance in the FMLA program that addresses what paperwork is needed to invoke the FMLA. Your medical history is no one's business but yours. Please refer to the Resources section to learn more about FMLA guidelines.

You can slow down the process of being on FMLA if you do not present all mandatory documents to your supervisor. To take time off for your health reasons or a family health issue, you want to invoke the FMLA as quickly as possible. If you need FMLA for more than thirty days, your employer can ask for additional medical certification for severe on-going health conditions. Your employer may only ask every thirty days for additional medical certifications. Per FMLA guidelines (§630.1208), you are required to provide the following information to your employer:

- The date the serious health condition commenced.
- The probable duration of the serious health condition or specify that the serious health condition is a chronic or continuing condition with an unknown duration and whether the patient is presently incapacitated and the likely duration and frequency of episodes of incapacity.
- The appropriate medical facts within the knowledge of the health care provider regarding the serious health condition, including a general statement as to the incapacitation, examination, or treatment that may be required by a health care provider.[75]

> **NOTE:** *It's particularly important to communicate your FMLA through email for documentation purposes. File your "email trail" in your binder. Stay organized. Be sure you ask your HR department who must sign your medical request to invoke FMLA; it is likely is a medical doctor or a nurse practitioner in most cases.*

From my experience of managing the FMLA program in my previous job, most employees' mistakes are incomplete forms and missing medical records. They may also have requested dates to take FMLA leave that do not match up with their doctor's recommendation of time they should be allowed to invoke FMLA leave. The US Department of Labor's Wage and Hour Division (WHD) is responsible for administering and enforcing the Family and Medical Leave Act for most employees.[76]

When you request to invoke FMLA, you also must state what type of leave or time off you are seeking. Will you use your sick leave, take vacation time or take leave without pay? I suggest you fully understand what is expected of you so you can use this valuable program when you need time off to heal and rest. I also encourage you to research the FMLA guidelines so you can read and understand what is required of you to use FMLA. You can get more answers to your questions on FMLA on the Department of Labor's website.[77]

NOTE: *Never abuse the FMLA, you could be held accountable. For example, it's not intended for vacations or pleasure travel. If someone is misusing FMLA for personal gain, it could backfire on the person who invoked FMLA. The Department of Labor's contact information is also in the resources chapter if you want to learn more about FMLA.*

If you are eligible to invoke FMLA because of your serious health issue, how could you use the time off to help yourself? For example, would you take naps and seek medical care. Would you also prepare your documentation that you may need to share with an attorney or other professional while you are at home? You can use this space or a separate piece of paper.

No FMLA in Your Company

If your company or organization does not offer FMLA, don't despair. Seek medical or professional care anyway. Be sure to give your employer as much notice as possible, as they may have to plan for you being away from the company. You may be eligible for filing a worker's compensation claim if workplace bullying or discrimination is harming your mental or physical health. You may also want to discuss this with an employment or labor attorney.

Worker's Compensation

If you can provide credible proof of documentation or witnesses that your employer created harmful stress that has affected your wellbeing, you may be eligible for worker's compensation. Each state has its guidelines on worker's compensation. Consider showing documented proof, such as medical records that reflect the physical or mental harm you are experiencing in the workplace. You may even want to discuss this further with an attorney.

Government employees can apply for a worker's compensation claim if they meet the following criteria according to the Department of Labor:

- The claim was filed within the time limits set by the Federal Employees' Compensation Act (FECA).
- The injured or deceased person was an employee within the meaning of the FECA. The injury, accident, or employment factor actually occurred, and a medical condition was diagnosed in connection with the injury or event.
- The employee was in the performance of duty when the event(s) leading to the claim occurred, and the medical evidence establishes that the diagnosed condition is causally related to the injury or event.[78]

Private sector employees should contact the designated official in their company to determine how to apply for worker's compensation. I encourage you to ask for references or the guidelines that your company is using for worker compensation. This way you can also know what you may be entitled to on this matter.

Employee Assistance Program (EAP)

The Employee Assistance Program (EAP) is a program designed to help employees find solutions to stress in the workplace, substance abuse, family issues, marital, financial, and other issues. If you have an EAP in your workplace, you may have access to medical advice by phone, legal assistance, adoption assistance, etc. In most cases, the EAP costs are paid for by the employer.

According to the Society for Human Resource Management (SHRM), situations in which an employer may mandate the use of an employee assistance program (EAP) are rare. The Employee Assistance Professionals Association (EAPA) in its Standards and Professional Guidelines indicate, "Employees may voluntarily seek EAP assistance or be referred to the EAP through constructive confrontation. Job security will not be jeopardized as a consequence of seeking or using EAP services, except where mandated by law."[79]

When an employer notices that there are performance issues with workers, especially when it's out of the norm, they may encourage them to seek assistance through the EAP. In most cases, you get to decide if you want to participate in an EAP. The good news is that the EAP is usually staffed with clinical social workers, substance abuse professionals, mental health counselors, and other professionals who can help you. Seeking assistance through an EAP could save hundreds or thousands of dollars since your employer will likely pay for it.

According to the *Houston Chronicle*, one of the cons of using EAP services are that they are technically supposed to be confidential, but this isn't always the case. Some EAPs are located in-house versus off-site. For example, if you are an employee walking into the EAP office for a voluntary counseling session that you don't want your colleagues to know about, but you have no control if a coworker sees you entering the office. There's not much you can do to maintain your privacy.[80]

From my experience working in HR, employees fear demotions, being denied a promotion, or stereotyped as a problem employee if they use their EAP. The best thing to do is to decide if this program is a good fit for you. Do you mind people knowing you are using an internal EAP or is your health and well-being more important? You can always seek professional medical care outside your workplace.

NOTE: *Be sure to check the resources section for more guidance on finding mental health support.*

In conclusion, there is a lot of information provided in this workbook to help you. You may find it useful to read it again and highlight "key" notes that you can refer back to and use. I have provided the same advice to my clients as you have read in this workbook. We all need to feel psychologically safe and to feel respected. Please check out www.WorkplaceBullyingSupport.com to read articles and listen to my syndicated radio show that supports safe and respectful work environments for employees and employers.

 RESOURCES TO HELP YOU

In this section, I have listed a variety of resources for you to check out. They have helped many people like you, who are looking for support.

Dawn Marie Westmoreland (author of this book) MM/HRM, CPC, CH

Dawn believes that employees and employers have the right to work in safe and respectful work environments. She is a workplace anti-bullying and discrimination speaker, author, coach, radio host, and HR consultant. Dawn has a master's degree in Management/Human Resources and is a certified Life Coach with iPEC. She is an advanced consulting hypnotist and is always learning new modalities to support her clients.

You can reach her at **www.workplacebullyingsupport.com**

Life Coaching

- Dawn Westmoreland is a certified Life Coach. She received her certification from iPEC in 2014. She works with clients to help them arrive to their personal goals around boundaries, bullying, discrimination, and personal power.
- If you are looking for a Life Coach, check out Institute for Professional Excellence in Coaching (iPEC) website: **www.ipeccoaching.com**

Equal Justice Initiative (EJI)

EJI confronts racial injustice, advocates for equality, and creates hope for marginalized communities. Attorney Bryan Stevenson is the founder and Executive Director of EJI in Montgomery, AL. **www.EJI.org**

Bullying/Whistleblowing

- Dawn Westmoreland provides consulting for bullying/discrimination, speaking, coaching, and books on workplace bullying. Check out **www.WorkplaceBullyingSupport.com**
- The National Whistleblowers Center (NWC) is a nonprofit, non-partisan organization that helps protect employees who disclose fraud, waste, and abuse. They sponsor advocacy, education, and assistance projects in a variety of program areas. **www.whistleblowers.org**

Discrimination

The US Equal Employment Opportunity Commission (EEOC) is responsible for enforcing federal laws that make it illegal to discriminate against a job applicant or an employee because of the person's race, color, religion, sex (including pregnancy, gender identity, and sexual orientation), national origin, age (forty or older), disability or genetic information. It is also illegal to discriminate against a person because the person complained about discrimination, filed a charge of discrimination, or participated in an employment discrimination investigation or lawsuit.

Most employers with at least fifteen employees are covered by EEOC laws (twenty employees in age discrimination cases). Most labor unions and employment agencies are also covered. The laws apply to all types of work situations, including hiring, firing, promotions, harassment, training, wages, and benefits. Check out **www.EEOC.gov** for more information.

Workplace Laws Not Enforced by the EEOC

Some workplace laws are not enforced by the EEOC; they are governed by different agencies. Here is a list that you can also find on the EEOC website, **www.eeoc.gov/laws/other.cfm**

The Civil Service Reform Act

The Civil Service Reform Act Of 1978 (CSRA): This law makes it illegal to discriminate against a federal employee or job applicant by race, color, national origin, religion, sex, age, or disability. The CSRA also prohibits discrimination by certain other factors that don't adversely affect employee performance, such as marital status, political association, and sexual orientation. The CSRA makes it illegal to fire, demote, or otherwise retaliate against a federal employee or job applicant for whistleblowing or for exercising the right to file a complaint, grievance, or an appeal. Check out **www.congress.gov/bill/95th-congress/senate-bill/2640**

Federal Prohibited Personnel Practices

The US Office of Special Counsel (OSC) is an independent federal investigative and prosecutorial agency. Our basic authorities come from four federal statutes: The Civil Service Reform Act, the Whistleblower Protection Act, the Hatch Act, and the Uniformed Services Employment & Reemployment Rights Act (USERRA). OSC's primary mission is to safeguard the merit system by protecting federal employees and applicants from prohibited personnel practices, especially reprisal for whistleblowing. **www.OSC.gov**

Federal Contractors

Executive Order 11246: This law makes it illegal for federal contractors and certain subcontractors to discriminate by race, color, religion, sex, or national origin. It also requires federal contractors and subcontractors to take steps to ensure equal employment opportunity in the workplace. For more information, contact the Department of Labor's Office of Federal Contract Compliance Programs (OFCCP) at 1-866-487-2365 (voice), 1-877-889-5627 (TTY), or visit **www.dol.gov/esa/ofccp**

Merit Systems Protection Board (MSPB)

The federal Merit Systems Protection Board (MSPB) exists to protect the rights of federal civil service employees. The MSPB is designed to be independent of partisan politics and to provide federal employees with an opportunity to appeal adverse and unfair personnel decisions. In order to fulfill its role as an independent and fair system, the MSPB has been carefully organized and its board members have been appointed by the President of the United States. Check out **www.mspb.org**

Civil Rights

- **Title VII of the Civil Rights Act Of 1964:** This law makes it illegal to discriminate by race, color, or national origin in programs and activities receiving federal financial assistance. For more information, contact the Department of Justice, Civil Rights Division at 202-514-2151 (voice), 202-514-0716 (TTY), or visit **www.justice.gov/crt/cor/coord/titlevi.htm**
- The Office for Civil Rights (OCR) is a sub-agency of the US Department of Education that is primarily focused on protecting civil rights in federally

assisted education programs and prohibiting discrimination on the basis of race, color, sex, national origin, sexual identity, age, handicap, or membership in patriotic youth organizations. **www.hhs.gov/civil-rights/index.html**

Americans with Disabilities Act

- **Title II of the Americans with Disabilities Act (ADA):** This law makes it illegal to discriminate against people with disabilities in all programs, activities, and services offered by state and local government agencies. This includes public transportation services and physical access to state and local government buildings. For more information, contact the US Department of Justice, Civil Rights Division, 800-514-0301 (voice), 800-514-0383 (TTY), or visit **www.doj.gov/crt/ada/adahom.1.htm**
- **Title III of the ADA:** This law prohibits disability discrimination by private entities that provide services to the public (also known as public accommodations. Public accommodations include, for example, restaurants, hotels, movie theaters, stores, doctors' offices, parks, and schools. For more information, contact the US Department of Justice, Civil Rights Division, 800-514-0301 (voice), 800-514-0383 (TTY), or visit **www.usdoj.gov/crt/ada/adahom1.htm**

Family Medical Leave Act

This law requires certain employers to grant up to twelve weeks of leave during a twelve-month period to eligible employees who need time off because of a serious health condition that they or someone in their family is experiencing. FMLA leave can sometimes overlap with Title VII requirements concerning leave for pregnancy and pregnancy-related conditions and ADA and Rehabilitation Act requirements concerning leave as an accommodation for an employee with a disability. For more information, contact the US Department of Labor, Employment Standards Administration, Wage and Hour Division, 1-866-487-9243 (voice and TTY) or visit **www.dol.gov/esa/whd/fmla**

Work Safety

OSHA's mission is to assure safe and healthful workplaces by setting and enforcing standards. They also provide training, outreach, education, and assistance. You can file a concern with them at 1-800-321-OSHA (6742). **www.OSHA.gov**

Rehabilitation Act

- **Section 503 of the Rehabilitation Act:** This law prohibits certain federal contractors and subcontractors from discriminating against qualified employees and job applicants with disabilities. Section 503 also requires contractors to take affirmative steps to hire and promote qualified people with disabilities. The non-discrimination provisions of Section 503 mirror those found in the ADA and Section 501 of the Rehabilitation Act. For more information, contact the US Department of Labor, Office of Federal Contract Compliance Programs, 1-866-487-2365 (voice), 1-877-889-5627 (TTY), or visit **www.dol. gov/esa/regs/compliance/ofcp/fs503.htm**
- **Section 504 Of the Rehabilitation Act:** This law prohibits disability discrimination in programs and activities that receive federal financial assistance. This includes discrimination against qualified applicants and employees with disabilities, as well as discrimination in the services and activities provided by federal agencies to the public. The non-discrimination provisions of Section 504 are similar to those found in Title I of the ADA, covering employment discrimination, and Title II of the ADA, covering the programs, activities, and services offered by state and local governments. For more information, contact the US Department of Justice, Civil Rights Division, 800-514-0301 (voice), 800-514-0383 (TTY), or visit **www.usdoj.gov/crt/ada/ adahom.1.htm**
- **Section 508 of The Rehabilitation Act:** This law requires federal agencies to ensure that electronic and information technology used by the government can be accessed and used by people with disabilities. For more information, contact the U.S. Access Board, 202-272-5434 (voice), 202-272-5449 (TTY), or visit **www.access-board.gov/**.
- Information can also be obtained from the U.S. General Services Administration, Center for IT Accommodation (CITA), 202-501-4906 (voice), 202-501-2010 (TTY), or visit **www.section508.gov**

Social Security

This law provides Social Security Disability Insurance (SSDI) to certain individuals with severe disabilities who can no longer work. The Social Security Act definition of disability is different from the ADA definition of disability. For this reason, whether or not you are eligible to receive disability benefits does not determine coverage under the ADA. For more information, contact the US Social Security Administration, 1-800-772-1213 (voice), 1-800-325-0778 (TTY), or visit **www.ssa.gov/disability**

Civil Rights

- The Office for Civil Rights (OCR) is a sub-agency of the US Department of Education that is primarily focused on protecting civil rights in federally assisted education programs and prohibiting discrimination on the basis of race, color, sex, national origin, sexual identity, age, handicap, or membership in patriotic youth organizations.
- The Fair Labor Standards Act regulates workplace practices related to minimum wage, overtime pay, and child labor. For more information, contact the US Department of Labor, Wage and Hour Division, 1-866-487-9243 (voice), 1-877-889-5627 (TTY), or visit **www.dol.gov/esa/whd**
- Department of Health & Human Services, Office for Civil Rights: at 1-877-696-6775 **www.hhs.gov/ocr/privacy/hipaa/understanding/special/genetic/index.html**

National Labor Relations Act

This law protects workers who wish to form, join, or support unions, or who are already represented by unions; and workers who join as a group (two or more employees) without a union seeking to modify their wages or working conditions. For more information, contact the National Labor Relations Board 1-866-667-NLRB (1-866-667-6572) TTY 1-866-315-NLRB (1-866-315-6572) **www.nlrb.gov/index.aspx**

Workers Compensation

Every state (and the federal government) has this law. It provides compensation for on-the-job injuries and illnesses. Some workers' compensation programs also require employers to provide job modifications or alternative assignments, which also may be a reasonable accommodation under the ADA. If an employee's occupational injury is covered under both Workers Compensation and the ADA (or Rehabilitation Act), the employee may be entitled to a job modification or reassignment under both laws. **www.dol. gov** (government employees) **www.nolo.com/legal-encyclopedia/free-books/employee-rights-book/chapter12-5.html** (for states)

Genetic (Hereditary) Information

Title I of Genetic Information Nondiscrimination Act: This title of GINA addresses the use of genetic information in health insurance. The provisions are enforced primarily by the Department of Labor's Employee Benefits Security Administration, with the Department of Health & Human Services' Office for Civil Rights enforcing Section 105 of Title I of GINA, which relates to GINA's protections for genetic information in the Health Insurance Portability Accountability Act privacy rule. For more information, contact the Department of Labor, Employee Benefits Security Administration at 1-866-444-EBSA (3272), 1-877-889-5627 TTY, **www.dol.gov/ebsa/consumer_info_health.html**

Mental Health

The National Institute of Mental Health (NIMH) is the lead federal agency for research on mental disorders. You can also find a mental health provider through this agency. **www.Nimh.nih.gov**

Spiritual

Martha Juchnowski, RN has practiced the healing arts for decades, as a Registered Nurse, teacher, and supervisor. After retiring from the nursing profession, she began practicing holistic healing while continuing her studies of energy healing, energy psychology, epigenetics, Spiritual Psychology, Quantum-Touch, Healing Touch, Matrix Energetics and Reiki. She is a certified 3rd level Reiki Master, spiritual counselor, and teacher and provides the energy work that supports a person's healing journey.

As an intuitive and medium, she can connect, when appropriate, to a person's guides (deceased loved ones or spiritual beings) who can help with one's journey. She also is an end-of-life counselor, provides energetic support during illness, treatments, and post-surgery. Contact her at MJuchnowski09@yahoo. com

Forest or Nature Therapy

Kathleen is a certified through the Association of Nature and Forest Therapy (ANFT) as a guide and Reiki master. You can reach her at **www.authenticofferings.com** or by email: kforrest@authenticofferings.com

Union or Trade Union

- National Education Association of the United States, which represents public school teachers and is the largest trade union in the United States. Check out: **www.nea.org/**
- Service Employees International Union, which represents hotels, restaurants, and hospitality workers; RNs, professional, technical and non-professional health care workers, and public employees. Check out: **www.seiu.org/**
- American Federation of State, County, and Municipal Employees, which represents employees of state, county, and municipal governments. Check out: **www.afscme.org/**
- International Brotherhood of Teamsters or Teamsters, which represents truck drivers, warehouse workers, and miscellaneous trades. Check out: **teamster. org/**
- United Food and Commercial Worker, which represents retail store and distribution employees. Check out: **www.ufcw.org/**
- Check out Federation of Teachers, which represents public school teachers, RNs, professional, technical and non-professional health care workers. Check out: **www.aft.org/**
- United Steelworkers, which represents steel mill workers and related trades. Check out: **www.usw.org/**
- International Brotherhood of Electrical Workers, which serves electrical manufacturing workers and electric utility workers. Check out: **ibew.com/**
- Laborers' International Union of North America, which represents miscellaneous construction workers and other trades. Check out: **www.liuna.org/**
- International Association of Machinists and Aerospace Workers, which represents aircraft manufacturing workers; aircraft maintenance and repair workers. Check out: **www.goiam.org/**

Department of Health and Human Services

US Department of Health and Human Services (HHS) prohibits discrimination by race, color, national origin, sex, age, or disability in certain health programs and activities. To be subject to these nondiscrimination rules, the health program or activity must receive federal financial assistance or be administered by certain governmental entities, including an administrator of the marketplace (the health insurance exchanges under the ACA). Although the guidance answers a number of questions raised by providers and health plan sponsors, it remains quite complicated in various respects. HHS will distinguish between discrimination caused by a third-party administrator's conduct and discrimination caused by an employer's plan design. **www.ballardspahr.com/ alertspublications/legalalerts/2016-05-26-aca-nondiscrimination-regulations-finalized.aspx** and **www.hhs.gov/**

USERRA/Military

USERRA protects civilian job rights and benefits for veterans and members of the active and Reserve components of the U.S. armed forces. USERRA provides that returning service-members must be promptly reemployed in the same position that they would have attained had they not been absent for military service, with the same seniority, status, and pay, as well as other rights and benefits determined by seniority. **www.dol.gov/vets/programs/userra/**

LGBTQI

The Human Rights Campaign and the Human Rights Campaign Foundation together serve as America's largest civil rights organization working to achieve LGBTQ equality. By inspiring and engaging individuals and communities, HRC strives to end discrimination against LGBTQ people and realize a world that achieves fundamental fairness and equality for all. They represent a force of more than 1.5 million members and supporters nationwide. As the largest national lesbian, gay, bisexual, transgender, and queer civil rights organization, HRC envisions a world where LGBTQ people are ensured of their basic equal rights and can be open, honest, and safe at home, at work, and in the community. **www.hrc.org/**

The National Gay & Lesbian Chamber of Commerce (NGLCC). The goal of NGLCC is to create an organization that could support LGBT business owners and showcases the diversity of talent in the lesbian, gay, bisexual, and transgender communities. NGLCC has succeeded in large part due to an amazing team and board combined with the caliber of businesses, corporate partners, and individuals that have become involved over the years. **www.nglcc.org**

Out & Equal. Partners with Fortune 1000 companies and government agencies to provide executive leadership development, comprehensive training and consultation, and professional networking opportunities that build inclusive and welcoming work environments. Since 1996, they have worked with executives, human resources professionals, Employee Resource Groups, and individuals to provide leadership and professional development, education, and research to create workplaces free of discrimination. **outandequal.org/**

Workplace Violence and Prevention

Felix Nater is one of the leading workplace violence prevention consultants. As he states, "A comprehensive workplace violence prevention assessment can help identify gaps in your workplace security posture, workplace policies, and culture that might create unintentional consequences and contributing factors." **www.naterassociates.com**

Human Resources Consultant

- Dawn Westmoreland provides employees and employers strategies to have respectful and civil work environments. She has thirty years' experience in Human Resources and a master's degree in Management/Human Resources. **www.WorkplaceBullyingSupport.com**
- Ryan McShane provides business leaders with the tools necessary to advance their company from a traditional business model to a "High Performance Leadership" model and empower employees to embrace the company's vision for the future. **hrevolutionllc.com**

Pro Bono and Reduced-Fee Legal Services

The United States Department of Justice provides a list of pro bono or reduced-fee legal service providers at **www.justice.gov/eoir/list-pro-bono-legal-service-providers** Also, be sure to inquire in your community for lawyers who offer legal advice pro bono, at a reduced rate, or on a sliding scale.

American Civil Liberties Union

For almost 100 years, the ACLU has worked to defend and preserve the individual rights and liberties guaranteed by the Constitution and laws of the United States. **action.aclu.org**

Behavioral Consultant

Jeff Riggenbach, PhD, is a best-selling author/speaker/coach with John Maxwell team. He is a behavioral consultant and trains companies on how to deal with high conflict personalities. You can reach out to Dr. Riggenbach and his team to start a conversation about your training needs at **DifficultPeople@JeffRiggenbach.com**

Employment Attorney

Stuart Silverman, Labor & Employment Law, Litigation, Corporate & Business Law Attorney Stuart Silverman has been practicing law in South Florida for over twenty-five years. His practice focuses on labor & employment, litigation, and business & corporate law. He can provide legal consultation to states outside of Florida and government cases. His extensive employment litigation experience includes claims under race, age, sex discrimination, wage and hour claims, ADA, and FMLA claims, whistleblower claims, public employee claims, and employment contracts. **www.linkedin.com/in/stuart-silverman-3515646**

 # EPILOGUE

I can provide guidance to you because I experienced severe bullying and discrimination. I gracefully have forgiven all my bullies for the harm they did to me. I learned a lot from my experiences, and I want to impart what I learned to others. I don't ever want anyone to suffer the consequences I experienced.

I have no animosity toward anyone who has ever mistreated me in the past. I look at them as part of my personal growth. I hope this workbook has enlightened and enriched your knowledge of how to stand up to workplace bullying and discrimination. You truly deserve to work in a safe and respectful work environment. Stay empowered!

If you need support that is not offered in this workbook, reach out to me through my website **www.WorkplaceBullyingSupport.com** I can't promise to answer every message I receive, but I will do my best to ensure that your questions are answered in future books or workbooks.

 # ENDNOTES

1 www.collective-evolution.com/2014/03/08/10-scientific-studies-that-prove-consciousness-can-alter-our-physical-material-world/

2 www.forbes.com/sites/lizryan/2016/06/26/five-reasons-not-to-care-what-your-boss-thinks/#55216aa93739

3 http://ethics.csc.ncsu.edu/old/12_00/basics/whistle/rst/wstlblo_policy

4 https://goodmenproject.com/featured-content/spending-a-morning-with-erin-brockovich-ndgt/

5 federalnewsradio.com/hiring-retention/2018/05/what-changes-and-doesnt-under-trumps-new-employee-removal-executive-order/

6 goodmenproject.com/featured-content/firing-federal-employees-quickly-maynot-be-good-thing-ndgt/

7 goodmenproject.com/featured-content/if-you-are-being-bullied-at-work-should-you-go-to-hr-for-help-ndgt/

8 www.psychologytoday.com/blog/intense-emotions-and-strong-feelings/201204/why-bullies-are-top

9 www.askmen.com/entertainment/special_feature_3700/3762_how-do-bullies-become-bullies.html

10 www.mindbodygreen.com/articles/14-signs-of-narcissism

11 www.business.com/human-resources/the-cold-hard-facts-about-workplace-bullying-and-how-to-handle-it/

12 www.usatoday.com/story/news/health/2013/10/08/hostile-workplace-less-productive/2945833/

13 www.psychologytoday.com/blog/wired-success/201105/the-silent-epidemic-workplace-bullying

14 www.eeoc.gov/employers/eeo-law-poster

15 www.eeoc.gov/eeoc/publications/immigrants-facts.cfm

16 www.psychologytoday.com/basics/bystander-effect

17 www.irs.gov/pub/irs-pdf/p4345.pdf

18 www.daveramsey.com/blog/the-truth-about-budgeting?snid=start.truth

19 www.eeoc.gov/wysk/recission-mandatory-binding-arbitration-employment-discrimination-disputes-condition

20 www.eeoc.gov/laws/types/retaliation.cfm

21 www.eeoc.gov/laws/types/index.cfm

22 www.eeoc.gov/laws/types/age.cfm

23 www.eeoc.gov/eeoc/newsroom/release/3-31-17.cfm

24 www.eeoc.gov/laws/types/disability.cfm

25 www.eeoc.gov/eeoc/newsroom/release/6-6-18c.cfm

26 www.ohchr.org/EN/Issues/Discrimination/Pages/discrimination_disabilities.aspx

27 www.eeoc.gov/laws/types/equalcompensation.cfm

28 www.eeoc.gov/eeoc/newsroom/release/11-15-17.cfm

29 www.eeoc.gov/laws/types/genetic.cfm

30 www.eeoc.gov/laws/types/genetic.cfm

31 www.eeoc.gov/eeoc/newsroom/release/11-1-16a.cfm

32 www.eeoc.gov/laws/types/harassment.cfm

33 www.eeoc.gov/laws/types/harassment.cfm

34 www.eeoc.gov/laws/types/race_color.cfm

35 www.eeoc.gov/eeoc/newsroom/release/2-1-18c.cfm

36 money.cnn.com/2015/11/25/news/economy/racial-discrimination-work/

37 www.eeoc.gov/laws/types/religion.cfm

38 www.eeoc.gov/eeoc/newsroom/release/6-20-18a.cfm

39 www.eeoc.gov/laws/types/religion.cfm

40 www.eeoc.gov/laws/types/sex.cfm

41 www.eeoc.gov/eeoc/newsroom/release/9-22-16a.cfm

42 www.eeoc.gov/eeoc/publications/upload/preventing_discrimination_lgbt.pdf

43 www.eeoc.gov/laws/types/pregnancy.cfm

44 www.eeoc.gov/eeoc/newsroom/release/7-2-18.cfm

45 www.eeoc.gov/laws/types/nationalorigin.cfm

46 www.eeoc.gov/eeoc/newsroom/release/10-3-16h.cfm

47 www.eeoc.gov/laws/types/sexual_harassment.cfm

48 www1.eeoc.gov/eeoc/newsroom/release/12-11-18.cfm?renderforprint=1

49 www.eeoc.gov/laws/types/retaliation.cfm

50 www.eeoc.gov/eeoc/newsroom/release/1-29-18a.cfm

51 en.wikipedia.org/wiki/Daniel_Ellsberg

52 www.zerohedge.com/health/veteran-cia-analyst-what-if-ignored-covid-19-warnings-had-been-leaked-wikileaks

53 www.eeoc.gov/federal/directives/md-110_chapter_7.cfm

54 www.hopkinsmedicine.org/health/wellness-and-prevention/sleep-answers-from-sleep-expert-dr-susheel-patil

55 www.webmd.com/anxiety-panic/guide/mental-health-hypnotherapy

56 www.massagetherapy.com/learnmore/benefits.php

57 www.stress.org/americas-1-health-problem

58 www.who.int/mediacentre/factsheets/fs369/en/

59 www.healthandyoga.com/html/meditation.aspx

60 liveanddare.com/types-of-meditation/

61 www.webmd.com/balance/stress-management/aromatherapy-overview#1

62 www.healthline.com/nutrition/what-are-essential-oils

63 www.verywellmind.com/what-is-art-therapy-2795755

64 www.mindbodygreen.com/0-23890/what-everyone-should-know-about-energy-healing.html

65 www.medicalnewstoday.com/articles/320019.php

66 www.ncbi.nlm.nih.gov/pubmed/22707959

67 www.nccih.nih.gov/health/chamomile/ataglance.htm

68 deliciousliving.com/supplements/6-herbs-and-supplements-reduce-stress

69 www.mayoclinic.org/healthy-lifestyle/consumer-health/in-depth/mindfulness-exercises/art-20046356

70 www.dol.gov/agencies/whd/fmla/faq

71 peoplesworld.org/today-in-labor-history-the-family-and-medical-leave-act-of-199/

72 www.dol.gov/whd/fmla/spouse/factsheet.htm

73 www.dol.gov/

74 www.dol.gov/whd/fmla/fmla-faqs.htm

75 www.federalregister.gov/documents/2000/05/08/00-11385/family-and-medical-leave

76 www.dol.gov/agencies/whd/fmla

77 www.dol.gov/whd/fmla

78 webapps.dol.gov/dolfaq/go-dol-faq.asp?faqid=371

79 www.shrm.org/ResourcesAndTools/tools-and-samples/hr-qa/Pages/cananemployerrequireanewhen employeetousetheservicesofaneap.aspx

80 work.chron.com/pros-cons-employee-assistance-program-12009.html,

 **NOTES**

Made in the USA
Columbia, SC
25 June 2021